THE LEGACY FAMILY WAY

HOW TO FOSTER FAMILY RELATIONSHIPS TO CREATE LASTING WEALTH

THE LEGACY FAMILY WAY

HOW TO FOSTER FAMILY RELATIONSHIPS TO CREATE LASTING WEALTH

Cindy Arledge

Praise for Cindy Arledge and
THE LEGACY FAMILY WAY

"Cindy has written an important book on the power of money to both build and destroy families. Her insights into money and values are especially helpful as families work together to navigate the difficult path of legacy, both with their resource of money, but also with the values they wish to pass down to generations. Cindy gives a blueprint for how to speak with family members about money and inheritance, before the death event occurs to help preserve family relationships. This book is the guide to having those difficult conversations now instead of at an emotionally charged, tense meeting in a lawyer's office. Use this book to plan ahead to save hurt feelings, misunderstandings and preserve family legacies."

—**Anne-Marie Faiola,** CEO and Founder, Bramble Berry ® Inc., and author of *Live Your Best Day Ever*

"Grief after death is expected, but the additional drama created by unprepared heirs is optional. Legacy Family Planning is the tool smart families use to protect their family's future."

—**Dean Lindsay,** author of *The Progress Challenge, Big Phat Goals*

"I wish that this book was available before my situation with my family crashed. Hopefully it will not be too late for you. This book is crammed full of good advice and easy to read."

—**Dennis De Naut,** World Traveler, Photographer of Light

"Cindy is both inspirational and cathartic. A general Wow! Now, I know where to go and what to do. Although it will evolve over time, I have a good starting point."

—**Don Rector,** Vice President, TPO Business Development, Caliber Home Loans

Praise for
CUR$E OF INHERITANCE

"I speak from experience when I counsel you to read and take to heart what you learn from this book. Ignorance is not bliss when it comes to inheritance. Adopting this information will not only change your life, it will improve the entire dynamic of your family."

—**Bobbi Schwartz,** Founder and CEO of Be Iconic Style

"My husband and I have been real estate investors for more than 20 years. We are all too familiar with the Cur$e of Inheritance. We've seen countless homes over the years owned by heirs of unplanned estates that end up in foreclosure or taken by the county for property taxes. The family ends up with broken relationships and no proceeds from what is often the most valuable portion of their loved one's estate. Over and over again they say, 'I never expected this from my siblings.'"

—**Toni D'Angelo-Lott,** HomeVestors, We Buy Ugly Houses™ Franchisee

"It isn't often we get simple advice for complex problems, but Cindy Arledge has managed to succinctly navigate the complexities of inheritance. Whether you are the beneficiary of an inheritance or the benefactor, this is a must read for the entire family. She writes from the heart and mind, and is straight forward and full of empirical data."

—**Kathy Miner,** Award-winning 5-Star Realtor

"A masterpiece that clearly defines wealth transfer conversations that families must have NOW to protect future relationships."

—**Lauren Midgley,** Time Behaviorist and author of *It's 6 a.m. and I'm Already Behind*

Praise for
My Camino, My Life

"Cindy's humorous and inspiring story is a great read for anyone considering walking the Camino or seeking more out of life."

—**John P. Strelecky,** #1 best-selling author of
The Why Cafe

"Cindy Arledge is a spirited & heart-centered entrepreneur. Her journey across the Camino is an inspiration. I admire her ability to turn grief into power. She can help you live with purpose, prosperity and joy."

—**Mastin Kipp,** best-selling author of
Daily Love: Growing into Grace

"I didn't know I needed the lessons, but they leapt from the pages and into my soul! I found myself smiling throughout the tale, and I could imagine myself right there with her. Cindy's insight and thoughts spoke to my heart and purpose."

—**Brenna Smith,** Founder and CEO
SheNOW, LLC

"Cindy takes you on a journey that will make you laugh, cry and think about your own path. Grab several copies and pass them out to all of the people you care about."

—**Kate Delaney,** Business Motivational Speaker
& NBC Talk Show Host

THE LEGACY FAMILY WAY
How to Foster Family Relationships to Create Lasting Wealth

Copyright © 2016 by Cindy Arledge
Published by: Legacy Inheritance Partners, Ltd
All Rights Reserved

5100 Eldorado Parkway, Suite 102-703
McKinney, TX 75070

All rights reserved. No part of this book may be reproduced in any form or by any means, electronic or mechanical, including photocopying, recording or by any information storage system without written permission from the publisher, except by a reviewer, who may quote brief passages in critical articles or reviews.

Cover design by Brian Moreland
Interior layout design by Brian Moreland
Illustrations by Lisa Rothstein
Graphic design by Maggie Hicks

The scanning, uploading, and distribution of this book via the internet or via any other means without the permission of the publisher is illegal and punishable by law. Please purchase only authorized electronic editions and do not participate in or encourage electronic piracy of copyrighted materials. Your support of the author's rights is appreciated.

ISBN 978-0-9826953-5-7

Disclaimer

This book is sold with the understanding that the publisher and author are not engaged in rendering legal, accounting or other professional services. Anyone planning to take action in any of the areas mentioned in this book should seek legal and expert assistance of trusted and competent professionals.

With the exception of the author's personal experiences, any similarity to actual people or places is coincidental. Names and places have been altered to protect confidentiality, and many stories are a compilation of actual experiences known to the author. Examples of Avoiders, Acceptors and Anticipators are the author's opinion only and are based on known facts concerning status of their will and behavior of family members after death.

Every effort has been made to make this book as complete and accurate as possible. However, there may be mistakes both typographical and in content. Therefore, this text should be used only as a general guide.

The purpose of this book is to educate, empower, and inspire action. The author and Legacy Inheritance Partners, Ltd shall have neither liability nor responsibility to any person or entity with respect to any loss or damage caused or alleged to be caused directly or indirectly by the information contained in this book.

Upon receipt of purchase, if you do not wish to be bound by the above, you may return this book to the publisher for a full refund.

Acknowledgments

Publishing a book sometimes feels like giving birth. After a long gestation period you make it through the birthing process and present your baby to the world. You don't know exactly what it will look like until it actually arrives. Each baby is different and special. Once you've been through the process and know what to expect, it gets easier each time.

My husband, Gerald, you are my rock. Your loving support has made it possible to write, edit and publish three books this year.

Thom Ricks, Jodi Stauffer, Kim Wallace and my fellow Artist Way Tribe members, thank you for nurturing the writer that was hiding inside me.

Lauren Midgley, I treasure your friendship, thank you for being you.

Brian Moreland, genius editor, thank you for working overtime to deliver this book on time. Your willingness to go beyond the call of duty is greatly appreciated.

To Maggie Hicks, your incredible talent, energy and joy for living are invigorating. Thank you for jumping on board to get this book done with Ease and Grace.

Lisa Rothstein, thank you for your continued support of this journey. Your cartoons continue to bring Legcacy Family Planning to life.

To Mike Koenigs and the PnP community! You are such an awesome group of committed authors. I am blessed to be a member.

Thank you to my family and friends who believe in me, when I forget to believe in myself.

*To my dad, E. K. "Sandy" Arledge and my belief,
that had you known about Legacy Family Planning,
you would have seen past your greatness to encourage it
in others, and by doing so, secured your lasting Legacy.*

"In the end, all that will matter is who you became. And how many you helped."

—Robin Sharma

Table of Contents

Introduction	1
Chapter One: The Real Issue	17
Chapter Two: The Solution	21
Chapter Three: Legacy Family Planning Basics	27
Part One - Foundation Phase	**45**
Chapter Four: Accept the Mantle of Leadership	47
Chapter Five: Identify Core Value Center	55
Chapter Six: Estate Plan Review	65
Part Two - Participation Phase	**75**
Chapter Seven: First Family Meeting	77
Chapter Eight: Pass the Torch	87
Chapter Nine: Create the Vision	97
Part Three - Creation Phase	**107**
Chapter Ten: Your Legacy Family Plan	109
About the Author	126
About the Illustrator	128

"The only true wisdom is in knowing you know nothing."

—Socrates

Introduction

Money is easy to make. Keeping it is harder to do. Lasting wealth, the kind of wealth that grows when passed from one generation to the next, is even more difficult to keep within the family. And until now, the ability to create generational wealth has been limited to a few ultra-wealthy families known as Legacy Families.

Why is it important to create lasting wealth? Actually, it's not. What's important is creating a pool of financial resources to invest in future generations' passionate expression of authentic gifts and talents to meet the world's needs while stewarding family funds in a family-first culture. In other words, teach your heirs how to create a satisfying, self-sustaining lifestyle, stay committed to each other, and grow their inheritance for the next generation. Let me explain.

Lasting wealth is merely the by-product of a family with the ability to steward family financial assets and retain family unity for multiple generations, like a modern-day clan. The Rothschild family exemplifies this idea. Amschel Rothschild was a poor Jew living in the Frankfurt, Germany Ghetto. When his parents died, he gave up his Rabbi training to return home to his brothers, married and raised ten children to adulthood. From these humble beginnings, the Rothschild family created an international financing business that continues today. The origination of the family wealth can be traced to the 1760s and remains under family control. Although the bank balances have ebbed and flowed over the centuries, the family culture remains intact.

Legacy Families are adept at creating generations of self-sufficient skilled members who desire to positively impact the world and pass their unique family wisdom and wealth from one generation to the next. Picture a single strand of thread. By itself, it is easy to break. But when threads are gathered together, their combined strength makes them almost impossible to cut. The more threads added to the strand, the greater the strength. This is the secret of Legacy Families.

To accomplish this herculean task, a plan, or covenant is created to provide governance for financial assets and guiding principles for family behavior. Think of it as a family constitution. This plan, covenant, or constitution, is the heart of the Legacy Family Plan.

To create a Legacy Family, you need:

1. A Family Founder with financial assets and a 100-year vision

2. The next generation, called the "Rising Generation", who is willing to accept stewardship of financial assets and take ownership of the family vision

3. A governance plan for assets and family members' agreement to honor a commitment to each other

4. Desire to be in service to others

Not everyone has a desire to create lasting wealth. They aren't concerned with a 100-year future, shared assets plans or business succession planning. They simply want to unite their family and ensure their financial gifts help their family, not destroy it. Some go through this process to prevent the Cur$e of Inheritance for their immediate family—their children and grandchildren. Others enjoy the process, the quality family time and transference of character and values. Family business owners have found the Legacy Family Planning Process to be a critical component of their succession plan. The list of Legacy Families throughout history is endless. Whether you have a small family with a few assets or a large, extended family with many assets and heirlooms, having a Legacy Family Plan in place will protect your heirs from disputes and lawsuits over their inheritance after you are gone.

Why is this important to me? My family was destroyed after my parents passed away eight months apart in 2005. By destroyed, I mean a brother who separated from the family and has yet to meet his grand-nieces and nephew, significant loss of my parents' hard earned assets, and my family's refusal to let go of misunderstandings in order to heal relationships.

Sadly, we are not alone. Few families are able to navigate the wealth transfer process with their family intact. Historically, statistically and worldwide, wealth is created and lost every three generations. In the U.S., we call it "shirtsleeves to shirtsleeves." In Ireland, it's called "clogs to clogs," and in Japan, it's called "rice paddies to rice paddies."

Why is this important to you? From my experience, it is the hope and dream of every loving parent to protect their family from harm, and provide, to the best of their ability, for their family's success. The challenge is how do you accomplish this goal? I have found the best way to succeed in life is to follow the best practices of successful people, then do what they do.

After my parents' deaths, I studied Legacy Families to determine what they do differently in order to understand what makes them successful. In the process, I discovered a tool for creating lasting wealth and realized it is the best kept secret hiding in plain sight. At the beginning of my research, I thought the secret to a Legacy Family's success was their incredible wealth. After digging deeper, I was ecstatic to discover success is, in large part, a function of the idea of stewardship and family-first culture.

And it makes total sense. Lasting wealth is the function of families who create wealth BUILDERS generation after generation, instead of wealth CONSUMERS. Lasting wealth is the by-product of strong families who commit to each other and grow family assets. I was thrilled to discover that you don't have to be super wealthy to be successful. There is hope for my children, and grandchildren, and those who will follow. There is hope for you and your family too.

This book provides a step-by-step approach to create your Legacy Family Plan, the best protection you can provide to prevent your family from being broke, bitter, and blaming you. The key to success is keeping an open mind, a willingness to adopt new ideas, and unwavering determination. At times, you may feel uncomfortable during the process, which is a normal part of change. The process of fostering deep family relationships is a lifelong endeavor. The by-product is lasting wealth for your family, and an incredible legacy for you.

My Story

I am the #1 best-selling author of *Cur$e of Inheritance*, founder of the Legacy Family Revolution, and the visionary leader of a new estate planning industry called Legacy Family Planning. My passion to help you and your family was born from the pain I experienced after my parents' deaths and the desire to protect my children and grandchildren from suffering the same.

I am bringing organization to the Legacy Family Planning industry so that others will not have to suffer as my family did when my parents passed away. I'd like to believe that if my parents had known about Legacy Family Planning they would have added it to the elaborate estate plan created by their attorney and CPA. And that my family would still be together, and the assets my parents worked so hard to earn would still be in our family.

Unfortunately, they didn't know about it. And in the decade since their death, a large portion of the assets they earned are no longer owned by family members. We have not celebrated a holiday together as a family since my parents' deaths, and several relationships remain severed.

In hindsight, based on the love we had for each other, I believe Legacy Family Planing would have prevented our family's destruction. We would have created a system with our parents, worked through our issues while they were still alive, and been prepared to become orphans. But, the reality is, I will never know because we didn't have the opportuntity. But I do know the Legacy Family Plan that Gerald and I introduced to our children has improved our relationsips. In addition, after I completed the first step, which is accepting the mantle of leadership, relationships with one of my brothers, several sisters-in-law, nieces and a nephew significantly improved as well.

In my last book, *Cur$e of Inheritance*, I shared the aftermath of my parents' estate plan. To summarize them here:

1. My father's fear of losing control of his assets resulted in $1,833,385.12 of estate taxes.

2. Dad changed his will, but Mom couldn't because of her Alzheimer's diagnosis. This resulted in their wills being incompatible for the grandchildren's portion of their estate.

3. To close the estate and honor my parents' desire for my children, I violated my personal value system to borrow millions of dollars for the purchase of commercial real estate. This transaction occurred a few months before the Crash of 2008 crippled the U.S. economy. Ouch!

4. In a fit of anger, Dad excluded a few members from his will, which destroyed the relationship between several sibling families that continues today.

In the wake of my parents' absence, I had to redefine myself, and in some ways, discover who I was for the first time. Looking back, I realize I never saw their stuff as ever belonging to me. In the two years between their deaths and the distribution of their estate, I was uncomfortable anticipating my inheritance. I was confused, so I began researching inheritance, prosperity and consciousness. I wanted to honor my parents and pass down their wealth to benefit future generations. I wanted their hard work and sacrifice to matter, to make the world a better place. The problem was,

I didn't know how to fulfill this desire until I discovered the following poem.

In the Crypts of Westminster Abbey, an Epitaph from the Tomb of an Anglican Bishop (AD 1100):

When I was young and free and my imagination had no limits, I dreamed of changing the world. As I grew older and wiser, I discovered the world would not change, so I shortened my sights somewhat and decided to change only my country.

But it, too, seemed immovable.

As I grew into my twilight years, in one last desperate attempt, I settled for changing only my family, those closest to me, but alas, they would have none of it.

And now, as I lie on my deathbed, I suddenly realize: If I had only changed myself first, then by example I would have changed my family.

From their inspiration and encouragement, I would then have been able to better my country and who knows, I may have changed the world.

This poem profoundly impacted me because it provided me with clear direction. The way to honor my parents and change the world was by changing myself. I studied universal laws and ancient wisdom from several sources and melded them into a set of ideas, beliefs, attitudes, practices and tools and created a formula for living that I call GRIPP Life™. GRIPP is an acronym for Gratefully, Responsibly, Intentionally Pursuing Purpose.

Using the GRIPP Life™ formula, I rebuilt my life. I felt prosperous despite the several million dollars of debt I had incurred. I stayed centered when my brother Richard was wrongfully convicted of conspiracy and sentenced to a federal prison for 16 years. I walked the Camino de Santiago, an ancient 500-mile pilgrimage across Spain over a period of 37 days with the intention of sharing the GRIPP Life™ formula upon my return.

Once home, I wrote my first book, *My Camino, My Life: A Sole to Soul Connection*. In doing so, I witnessed my own healing in the writing process. My plan to share the GRIPP Life™ formula was replaced with an urgency to prepare my family to receive their inheritance and warn others of the danger surrounding failed inheritances. My second book, *Cur$e of Inheritance*, became a #1 best seller that launched the Legacy Family Revolution. And in this book, I am sharing the best practices of successful wealth transfer so you can create your Legacy Family Plan to protect your family's future.

Before You Begin . . .

If you are like most people, you haven't heard of Legacy Families or Legacy Family Planning. Until recently, Legacy Family Planning was reserved for ultra-high-net-worth families with access to the "Family Office" industry. Utilizing trained professionals to support their family's wealth is one way to keep wealth in the family. Like a business, these families create a team of advisors, similar to a Board of Directors (BOD), to serve their family. Although the Legacy Family Planning industry isn't new, for the majority of the population, its existence is virtually unknown.

My passion is to increase the awareness for this industry, and educate families to the benefits of adding Legacy Family Planning to their estate plan. As baby boomers die over the next thirty years, more than 30 trillion dollars are expected to be transferred to the next generation.

Sadly, based on historical data, 85% of these wealth transfers will result in failure. By failure, I mean destruction of family relationships, loss of financial capital, and unnecessary upheaval for family members. No parent wants this for their children, or their grandchildren. Until now, the tools to prevent this from happening have been reserved for high-net-worth families. With so many families at risk, now more than ever, it's time to take action to prevent this impending tragedy.

What is Legacy Family Planning?

Legacy Family Planning fills the gap between traditional estate planning professionals. Your attorney creates the legal documents, your Certified Public Account creates your tax plan, and your wealth managers provide wealth advice. Until now, you didn't have an experienced advisor to help you prepare your family. I'm not talking about therapy. Legacy Family Planners leave that to licensed counselors. Legacy Family Planners are trusted and trained advisors who help families prepare the heart-centered group of documents that serves as a guide for the other plans and offers the best protection for their families.

So, what do Legacy Family Planners do?

Legacy Family Planners are trained, trusted advisors who have personally been through the Legacy Family Planning process with their own family. They have completed training, passed a certification test, and agreed to abide by a professional code of conduct. They have your family's best interest in mind at all times. The best planners have cultivated a team of professionals in a variety of fields to assist you and your family in the implementation of your Legacy Family Plan.

Every family has issues, it's a part of the human condition. The list of situations that creates underlying tension in a family is endless. From unresolved conflicts, smoldering childhood resentments, and/or separation caused by distance, differences in lifestyle and values, to abuse, chronic illness, criminal behavior, drugs, addiction, death and/or mental illness.

How family members react and respond to these situations are affected by their family position (oldest, middle, baby of the family), temperament, emotional IQ, personality, education, strengths, health, lifestyle and a myriad of other variables. Legacy Family Planners cultivate a team of professionals to assist the family when situations arise outside the expertise of the planner.

Why, with best practices of professional support, and undeniable complications of family dynamics, do I provide this information to you in a do-it-yourself (DIY) format? There are several reasons.

First, I want to make this information easily available. Although families from all economic situations benefit from creating a Legacy Family Plan, I've found that financially successful families and business owners are the ones most willing to take action. Having survived the nightmare of a failed inheritance, I am passionate about sharing this revolutionary solution in an affordable and efficient way so that any family who wants access to the information can find it through my books and supporting websites.

Second, it's not the size of the inheritance that destroys a family, it's unprepared heirs. Anyone who is interested in protecting their family's future can follow the step-by-step process in this book. I know, because I've done it. Although my depth of Legacy Family Planning is helpful, our blended family has issues to navigate like everyone else. Our ability to communicate with honesty and vulnerability has improved and it feels like we are building a bridge to our future as we go.

If, after reading this book, you choose to hire a Legacy Family Planning advisor instead of doing it yourself, you will be better educated, which will enable you to choose the best advisor for your family. Just like an attorney can help you with legal advice and a financial planner can advise you on investing, a Legacy Family Planner can help you avoid common mistakes, be an outside resource for your family and indicate your level of commitment to your family. There is no badge of honor handed out for taking the hard road in life, so I hope you will consider adding a Legacy Family Planner to your estate planning team. For most families, utilizing the services of a professional Legacy Family Planner is the best path to success. If you choose the DIY method, this book provides basic information to complete your Legacy Family Plan.

Dear reader, my assumptions about you . . .

As the author, I made the choice to present this information from a narrow perspective with a few assumptions about you that include:

1. You are a parent or grandparent of adult children.

2. You have excess assets you intend to leave your family.

3. You already have a will or estate plan in place.

In other words, like me, you are expected to die in the next 30 to 50 years. Our combined 30 trillion dollars will bless or destroy our families based on the actions we take, or don't take, to protect them now. History has proven that traditional estate planning isn't enough to protect our family. Now is the time to utilize the best practices of Legacy Families to protect our family's future.

What about readers who are young and have a long life ahead of them? Don't worry, you will also benefit from this book. In fact, many times you will find it easier to create your plan than those who are already grandparents.

Here's why. If you are single, newly married or parents of young children, you won't have adult children to ask for input on your plan. This simplifies the process considerably. For now, it's just you, and/or you and a spouse. If you have young children, they will grow up with the positive influence your Legacy Family Plan provides and readily accept it as part of your family culture. Or, perhaps you are the adult child of a patriarch or matriarch who doesn't have a Legacy Family Plan in place. This information could save your family.

And if you don't have excess assets yet, a Legacy Family Plan might be just the encouragement you need to begin putting money aside. Even without assets to bequeath, your family will benefit from all other aspects of the plan. If you are expecting an inheritance in the future, now is the time to prepare to receive it so that it will be a blessing for you and your family.

But, if you don't have an estate plan in place, you will need to get it done as part of your Legacy Family Plan. Without a valid will, your Legacy Family Plan is doomed to fail. My previous book, *Cur$e of Inheritance*, is an excellent reference to understand the importance of facing the topic of death.

If you don't currently have a will, please know you are not alone. According to a 2014 *Forbes* article, 51% of Americans between the ages of 55 and 64 don't have a will. Men are more likely to have a will than women. When considering younger age groups, the number of people without a will dramatically increases to 64% who lack protection.

Many people don't know what a will is, or how to get one, so *now* is a good time to get on the same page about the term "will." For the purposes of this book, "will" is a group of essential estate planning documents that, at a minimum, contain the following: (1.) Last Will and Testament, (2.) Statutory Power of Attorney, (3.) Power of Attorney for Health Care, and (4.) DNR-Do Not Resuscitate. Depending on your family's needs, your situation may require additional documents. And, just in case you missed the disclaimer, I'm repeating myself here, because it is important that you know: this book does not provide legal advice. Please, contact your professional advisors for legal advice.

The format of this book was inspired by two of my favorite Julia Cameron books, *The Artist's Way* and *The Prosperous Heart*. When Julia wrote *The Artist's Way*, she was advised to limit the availability of her information to exclusive classes. But Julia refused, and by putting her content into book form, she has helped millions of readers around the world embrace a creative and prosperous life, including me. My greatest desire in sharing this content in book format is to inspire millions of families to implement a Legacy Family Plan to foster family relationships and create lasting wealth.

How to Read This Book

Like *Cur$e of Inheritance*, this book is easy to read. I suggest you read the book in its entirety once, before beginning the process. After the initial read you will have a thorough understanding of the process and can make an educated decision on what's right for you and your family. For your convenience, I've added a note section at the back of this book to capture your ideas.

If you decide to engage the services of a Legacy Family Planner, this book will provide you with a point of reference to help you during the process. If you decide to DIY, an initial read enables you to move through the process with confidence and schedule your time wisely. It doesn't matter how you create your plan, it only matters that you do. Become the "Family Founder" and protect your family from their biggest threat, themselves.

> *"The journey of a thousand miles begins with one step."*
>
> **—Lao Tzu**

"You're either part of the solution or you're part of the problem."

—Eldridge Cleaver

Chapter One: The Real Issue

This chapter asks that you open your mind and think about death and money in a new way. For the vast majority of people, death is a topic to avoid. Not surprisingly, avoidance is at the heart of the problem. Sadly, society has accepted failed inheritances as normal. By breaking the taboo on discussing death and money, you will gain understanding of the real issue and access to a viable solution. Open your mind to a new viewpoint, to discover the solution.

To find the solution, you must first understand the problem.

If you don't understand the real problem, you can't find the real solution. Rather than regurgitate the contents of *Cur$e of Inheritance*, I am including a few key concepts. You don't need to read *Cur$e of Inheritance* to successfully create your Legacy Family Plan, but doing so will provide you with a deeper understanding.

Inheritance failures are not caused by wealth (or money). Money does contribute and complicate the problem, but it doesn't cause the problem. **Money is neither good nor bad, it is amoral.** The real problem is our avoidance of death and failure to prepare our heirs for life without us. When we resist, avoid and ignore the one thing that life guarantees, we put our family in danger.

Money contributes to the problem because it amplifies who we are and our relationship with it. If your heir is generous, more money will make them more generous. If your heir is greedy, more money will increase their greediness.

To complicate the problem, unearned wealth received by unprepared heirs is cursed. Things obtained without effort come with a spiritual attachment. The Kabbalists call it "the Bread of Shame." It's more commonly referred to as "a free lunch." The Bread of Shame is a little known, but powerful force. Just ask any lottery winner!

Our current culture doesn't recognize the real problem. While many grumble and shake their heads, the sad truth is that society has accepted failed inheritances as normal. Between the taboo nature of death and money, lack of understanding the real issue, and no viable solution, without a revolution, the proliferation of broken families will continue.

The cause of the problem is avoidance of death and failure to prepare heirs. The effect of the problem is failed inheritances. Remember, money amplifies and unearned money is cursed. If you are not prepared, and someone has to die for you to receive money, presumably someone you loved, the money can feel dirty. Leaving money to unprepared heirs unleashes an insidious form of the Bread of Shame that I now know is the Curse of Inheritance.

The Cur$e of Inheritance

The Cur$e of Inheritance is an ugly monster of jealousy, fear and selfishness that crushes families, eats money and destroys lives. The Cur$e of Inheritance is born in an environment of loss and grief, by unprepared heirs who feel entitled to unearned wealth and forget to see each other as human beings.

Understand the problem, then find the solution.

Now that the problem is clearly defined, let's move on to the solution. Keep in mind that lasting wealth is the by-product. The real goal is the long-term success for your family, both now and in the future. Having the courage to plan and prepare for your death is one of the three pillars that lasting wealth is built upon. We are talking about your legacy.

All truth passes through three stages.

First, it is ridiculed. Second, it is violently opposed.

Third, it is accepted as being self-evident."

—Arthur Schopenhauer

Chapter Two: The Solution

Now that the problem is clearly defined, it's time to introduce you to the solution and explain why traditional estate planning isn't enough to protect your family. You will have an opportunity to complete an assessment to determine your location on the Estate Planning Pyramid, as well as your family's expected outcome. Your position on the pyramid determines their future.

The Three Pillars of Lasting Wealth

Lasting wealth is built on three pillars of strength. The illustration below clearly shows why so many wealth transfers fail. Between the cultural taboo of death and money, and previous lack of access to Legacy Family Planning, families have been relying on just two pillars to transfer their wealth. It is little wonder why 85% of inheritances fail.

As you can see, traditional estate planning that focuses on Legal Documents to distribute Financial Assets and other possessions doesn't provide the necessary support to successfully transfer wealth. The focus of this book is the third pillar of Legacy Family Planning. The pillars of Legal Documents and Financial Assets, etc. are outside the scope of this book.

The first pillar, **Legal Documents**, provides your family the authority they need to execute your last wishes. It is why I stressed the importance of obtaining a will earlier. Without the protection of legal documents, your family is exposed to unnecessary and avoidable pain and agony. Inheritances are determined in the courtroom arena, and without the necessary legal documents, your family doesn't have the tools they need. The state you live in will determine how to divide your estate. Your legal documents are the first pillar of lasting wealth.

The second pillar, **Financial Assets, etc.**, are the financial resources and physical possessions you leave behind. Many believe this is the most important pillar because they are tangible, and the subjects of disagreements, lawsuits and broken relationships. Families who are unaware of Legacy Family Planning and how to become an Anticipator rely on Legal Documents to transfer their financial assets and other possessions.

The third pillar, **Legacy Family Plan**, is the plan, or covenant that allows you to create a unified family of skilled members who desire to positively impact the world and pass their unique family wisdom and wealth from one generation to the next. Your Legacy Family Plan is the first line of defense for the Cur$e of Inheritance. This is where you build a foundation of gratitude and stewardship to replace entitlement. This is where you build trust and communication to replace jealousy, fear and selfishness.

Be an Anticipator

Building strong pillars is the key to creating lasting wealth. If you have not read *Cur$e of Inheritance* you may not be familiar with the term **Anticipator**. In it, I introduced the three levels of the Estate Planning Pyramid (EPP). The EPP consists of two sides with three levels each. The left side of the pyramid measures your personal level of death preparation. The three levels are **Avoider, Acceptor** and **Anticipator**. The right side of the pyramid predicts your family's future based on your preparation. The three levels are **Lost, Limited** and **Legacy**. The better prepared you are for death, the more favorable outcome you can expect for your family.

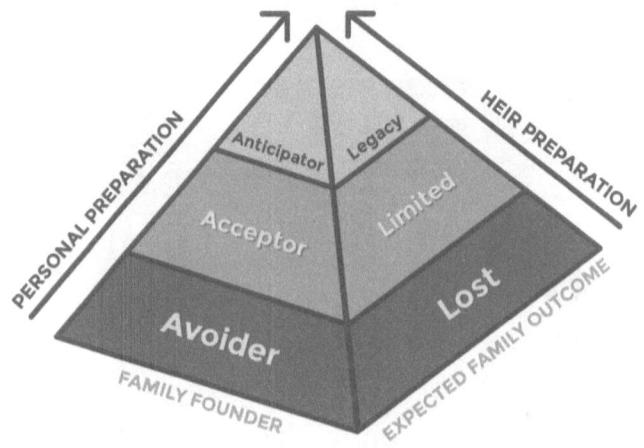

To determine your location on the EPP, download a printable copy of Estate Planning Pyramid at **www.LegacyFamilyRevolution.com/assessment**. It doesn't matter if you are an Avoider or Acceptor, you can become an Anticipator and create a Legacy family.

Prepare for your Legacy Family Plan by seeing your inheritance through the eyes of your beneficiaries. The more thorough your ability to anticipate how your absence will affect them, the better you can prepare them for life after you are gone. Prepare your heirs now so that they won't suffer from the Cur$e. The key to protecting your family's future is your willingness to be uncomfortable with facing your own mortality. Be an Anticipator to build a strong third pillar of lasting wealth.

Legacy Family Plan, the Third Pillar of Lasting Wealth

Creating a Legacy Family Plan is a three-phase process that includes Foundation, Participation and Creation. Fair warning, creating the plan is just the beginning. The final step, Creation, is an ongoing process of implementation, measurement and adjustment that is transferred from one generation to the next. It becomes a way of life that enriches conversations, deepens relationships and builds unity within the family. Creating a Legacy Family Plan is the third pillar of lasting wealth.

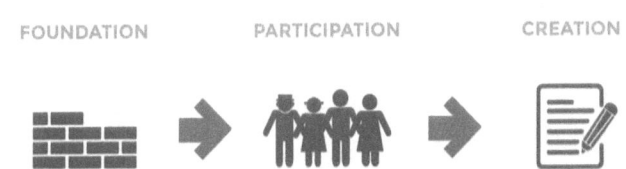

In the Foundation Phase, the first phase, you will accept the mantle of family leadership, discover your core values and complete an estate review. In the Participation Phase, the second phase, you will invite the rising generation to the process and introduce them to the concept, discover their strengths, motives, ask them to participate and co-create a vision for the future. In the Creation Phase, the third and final phase, you will draft, adopt and implement your Legacy Family Plan. Implementation is a lifelong process that builds trust and communication with a key ingredient of having fun together! Ironically, your Legacy Family Plan is built around anticipating your death.

The rest of this book is dedicated to helping you become an Anticipator and assisting you in the creation of your Legacy Family Plan. Build a strong pillar to protect your family and create lasting wealth for your family. During the process, you will be working with your other advisors to create your Board of Directors and make any adjustments needed on the other two pillars.

"No problem can be solved from the same level of consciousness that created it."

—Albert Einstein

Chapter Three:
Legacy Family Planning Basics

In this chapter you will learn that legacy and inheritance are not the same. In addition to hearing my dad's story, you will discover the importance of investing in the four capital accounts, and how 21 key characteristics provide a foundation for your Legacy Family Plan. Finally, you will hear the cautionary tale of my friend, Buddy.

Legacy vs. Inheritance

It is important to understand the difference between legacy and inheritance. Legacy is seen through your eyes. Inheritance is seen through the eyes of your beneficiaries. The best way to prepare your heirs is to see life through their eyes and anticipate the impact that your passing will have on their life, as well as how your financial gifts will affect them. Money is an amplifier. An inheritance will increase their current relationship with money. Legacy Family Planning is the tool that allows you to prepare your heirs to continue building your legacy by growing their skills, and encouraging them to fully embrace their authentic self. Do it while you are alive so you can enjoy their growth.

What would Sandy say?

As a writer, information is often "downloaded" in the middle of the night, driving down the highway or while taking a shower. Or, in my case, a hot bath. Inspiration can be found anywhere, from real life, fiction, or voices in my head.

During the development of this book, I could hear Dad's voice from two distinct points of view. The first perspective came from the man I loved, respected and accepted for who he was. We didn't always agree, but we learned how to move past our disagreements.

The second perspective came from my guardian angel, the one who continues to care for my family from the other side. This is the perspective that sees the benefits of Legacy Family Planning and expressed regret for failing to protect his family. Receiving a message of regret after he was gone was both surprising and encouraging. One of Dad's favorite sayings was, "Regret is the most wasted emotion that exists. You can't change the past." This message provided encouragement to help others who face a similar situation, because I understand power-motivated wealth builders and their legacy challenges.

I am not implying that I'm a medium. I'm not. But I do know that relationships don't always end when someone dies. When the connection is strong, the relationship continues, one way or the other. My middle brother's relationship with Dad remains strong, but sadly, his is one of bitterness and blaming of a dead man that has become a sad way of life.

My experience has been entirely different. Navigating debt during the economic meltdown increased my appreciation for Dad's business skills. Over the past decade, I've asked myself more than once, "What would Dad do?" Within a few days, an idea would pop into my head that felt right. Taking action on these ideas allowed us to survive the economic crisis. I am positive that Dad's spirit continues to look out for me. After asking for guidance and receiving an answer, I have learned how to trust the responses I receive.

Dad's nickname was Sandy, and he reminds me of a Texas version of John Wayne and the wonderful characters he portrayed. Tall, handsome, outspoken, headstrong, and when he wasn't being stubbornly independent or a bully, he was charming and entertaining. People either loved him or hated him; there were no in-betweens.

Dad was the product of a broken home during the Great Depression. Sorting through old pictures, his sisters showed me the houses he grew up in that didn't have running water or electricity. At 19, he married my mother, and in less than ten years they were raising four children. During his lifetime he worked hard, took risks, and many claimed he had the Midas touch. When he passed away at 76, he had accumulated a portfolio of commercial properties and a fistful of broken relationships.

Dad was fully aware of the problems that existed in our family but didn't know how to address them. Rather than face this lack of ability, he took the easy way out and changed his will. He knew his decisions would create havoc and apologized to me in advance.

Our family didn't qualify for support from the Family Office industry, and didn't know about Legacy Family Planning. Had Dad known about it, based on the perspective of Sandy, the man I knew growing up, the invitation to sit down to address these broken relationships would probably have sounded like this, "Cindy, this is @%*#! There is no way I'm going to talk to these ungrateful @%*#!... Let them rot in @%*# for all I care."

Not all financially successful families have Type-A personalities at the helm. In today's world, technology has given entrepreneurs the ability to create enormous wealth and enjoy healthy work/life balance. Especially among the Millennials. If this is you and your family, congratulations! If you think you don't need Legacy Family Planning because everyone appears to "get along," don't fool yourself. You cannot anticipate how your family will respond to their inheritance until after it happens. And then, it's too late. Adding a Legacy Family Plan to your estate plan is the best protection you can provide for your family's future.

Can you relate to my dad's perspective? If your wealth creator is anything like Sandy Arledge was, success in business doesn't necessarily translate into successful relationships at home. Sadly, this failure on the home front accounts for the majority of inheritance failures. If your dynasty builder shares Sandy's "do it my way or hit the highway" attitude, it is even more important for you to add Legacy Family Planning to your estate plan.

My guardian angel's perspective sounds like this: "Honey, if I'd only known, I would have done things differently. We could have avoided the mess I put you through. Tell our story to help others avoid this disaster so others can avoid this pain and suffering."

The insight I gained from the two perspectives enabled me to recognize that Dad only wanted the best for his family, and he did the best he could with the information he had available to him at the time. His behavior was the result of his childhood background, life experiences, ego, motive and personality. I've lived the nightmare. Please allow me to assist you in protecting your family from a similar disaster.

The Capital Competency List and Four Capital Accounts

Traditional estate planning uses legal documents to distribute assets. Focus is typically limited to the distribution of *financial* assets. Many times, financial rewards are used as incentives for "good" behavior. Clearly, this system is not working.

Legacy Family Planning is quite different. Financial assets are invested in the education and training of family members to achieve a high level of competency in four capital accounts. These accounts include financial, intellectual, social and human capital. A list of essential skills in each of the capital accounts are compiled in the Capital Competency List.

The Capital Competency List provides focus for educating family members and provide opportunities to EXPERIENCE lessons to become competent in the skills listed on the Capital Competency List. It is critical to create a safe environment to make mistakes. Mistakes are opportunities for growth and learning.

So what are capital accounts and what do they do?

Let's start with **financial capital**. In its most simple form, you can measure your financial capital by measuring your net worth. The greater your net worth, the more choices you have in life. Your financial capital is the resource that provides choices in life.

Intellectual capital includes innate learning styles and the collective knowledge you possess. Knowing your learning style and creating a lifelong learning goal is one way to increase your intellectual capital. Investing in family members' competencies increases the family's capital account, which benefits the family by creating a depth of intellectual capital to make better decisions.

Social capital is defined as the amount of "collective good" you provide with the time, talent and treasure you donate in service to others. Measuring "collective good" gives you a tool to make informed decisions on the highest and best use of your valuable resources. Measuring and comparing are the keys to obtaining the highest impact for your donation, whether it is time, talent or treasure. Giving to others increases gratitude, which is the antidote to entitlement.

Human capital is the accumulation of health, emotional intelligence, skills, personality, intellectual capital and motivation. Business owners invest in their people because it increases the value of their business. Employee development leads to increased productivity, which leads to higher profits. Human capital development is the heart and soul of the Legacy Family Planning process.

Decades before I knew about Legacy Families, I was unknowingly providing capital account training for my daughters. Quite the opposite of ultra-wealthy families, the opportunities I provided were born from necessity. As a single mother of two pre-teenage girls, I struggled with the escalating cost of their social life. Their dad sent child support each month, just not always in a timely manner. As the daughter of a retired banker, fiscal responsibility is something I value, and despite late child support payments, I was determined to pay my bills on time.

After reviewing my expenses, I discovered, to my horror, that I spent more on my children's friends' gifts than I did for my own daughters' gifts. After a spark of inspiration, I decided to give the majority of my child support checks to the girls, letting them use the money to pay for their incidental expenses: haircuts, school lunches, entertainment, birthday parties and clothes.

The first month, they were thrilled. They thought they were rich! Then, reality set in. Those cute designer jeans cost more than their monthly clothing allowance. And that friend of a friend's birthday party next week, meant money out of their pocket, not mine. Faced with the freedom to choose how to spend their money, they EXPERIENCED the consequences of choice. While I was taking care of the BIG STUFF, like the house, electricity, car and insurance, they were learning how to juggle priorities with the small stuff.

Requests for more money were denied. When I wouldn't relent, they became masters of creative solutions. They fixed a sack lunch at home and spent their lunch money elsewhere. A new prom dress? I don't think so. They swapped prom dresses with friends before it was popular to do so.

My youngest daughter caught on quickly, and remains one of the best money managers I know. When my oldest called from her freshman college dorm and said, "I get it, Mom. You won't believe how my classmates are charging up their credit cards and don't know how to handle their money," I smiled.

We all benefitted from this decision. My ex-husband was happy to see his money going directly to the girls. If he was late, which wasn't often, they were like tax collectors, hounding him for their allowance. There were no more arguments about what I would and would not buy. By far, the girls benefitted the most because they learned how to manage money in a safe environment.

Developing human capital at the family level is the secret tool that Legacy Families use to create lasting wealth. They have discovered that fostering family relationships, a human capital investment, is the key to preventing inheritance problems in the future. Teaching conflict resolution, communication and emotional intelligence skills at the family level creates a unified, family-first culture.

The Capital Competency List provides focus and accountability for training family members. Each generation is provided education, opportunities to experience lessons, and a safe environment to make mistakes. The Capital Competency List is a curriculum to achieve a high level of competency in essential life skills in the financial, intellectual, social and human capital accounts.

The Capital Competency List provides a skills checklist to invest in the education and training of family members. The necessary skills to *own your life* are built upon a foundation of 21 key characteristics.

21 Key Characteristics

Life is your job and your *family is your business*. When you see life through this lens, success looks different. Success is measured by self-fulfillment instead of income, investments or accumulated toys. My father's dual perspectives gave me the courage to share this information when others suggested that the topic was too controversial, too personal, and not what people want to hear.

Everyone has the right to decide what makes them feel fulfilled. Whether it's teaching, raising children or owning their own business. Legacy Families encourage an inside-out approach to life by encouraging children to pursue their dreams, and their authenticity.

The 21 Key Characteristics provide the framework for consistently transferring the ability to create a life based on happiness from the inside, independent of financial success. This approach means that happiness is not determined by external conditions. Each generation is inspired to express their authentic passion, purpose and willingness to fund their own lifestyle through investing in the family's Capital Competency List curriculum and the framework provided by the 21 Key Characteristics.

When you accept life as your job, and your family as your business, your business becomes the transference of *living your legacy*. I'm not talking about transferring your financial assets and other possessions, I'm talking about a system to transfer a meaningful life of passion by investing in the skills development for your family members.

www.LegacyFamilyRevolution.com

Financially Savvy - The ability to be financially independent, manage, grow and protect wealth, including familiarity with accounting principles and the ability to monitor advisors.

Stewardship of Resources - Stewardship is more than putting money aside. It is living within your means, being grateful for what you have, and investing in your values. It is the wise use of resources, and a "caring for" instead of an "ownership" perspective.

Competent - Financial resources are invested to develop competencies in the four capital accounts according to a list of necessary skills defined in the covenant.

Authentic - We are born with our core motivation and personality traits intact. Investing in the development of authenticity develops our unique gifts and talents.

Purpose - Purpose can be as simple as following Joseph Campbell's advice to "Follow your bliss."

Service - Life without service to others lacks meaning. Gifts and talents are to be shared to meet the world's needs. Doing so increases gratitude and fulfills our life's purpose.

Gratitude - This is the foundation. Gratitude is the antidote to entitlement. Entitlement is a form of anger, specifically tied to unmet expectations. Creating and transferring an attitude of gratitude is fundamental to the Legacy Family Planning process.

Delayed Gratification - This characteristic is vital for success. The Stanford *Marshmallow Test* has proven that people who are able to delay gratification are more likely to succeed.

Consciousness Mind-set - Rise above poverty, middle class and wealth money mind-set to consciousness level. Pay attention to the voices in your head. Separate yourself from your ego and embrace Consciousness.

Inside-Out Approach - Happiness is an inside job, but so is being miserable. The choice is ours, and ours alone, to make. With an inside-out approach, the solution is always found within and is not reliant on external circumstances.

Responsible - Acceptance of personal responsibility gives us power. When we attempt to take responsibility for others, or make others responsible for us, we give our power away. We are only responsible for ourselves, not for other competent adults.

Congruent - When our time, checkbook and behaviors align, we are congruent with our beliefs. When we are congruent, words and actions match. We become the living embodiment of our values.

Belief That Everyone Is Doing Their Best - This characteristic is easy for people to express when they believe they are doing their best. The opposite is true. People who don't believe they are doing their personal best fail to see it in others.

Embrace Mistakes - Mistakes are learning and growing opportunities with appropriate consequences. When it is safe to make mistakes, it is easier to believe that you are doing the best you can in any given situation.

Curious - We can never really know what someone else is going through, or what they need, unless we ask. Curiosity in place of assumptions fosters healthy relationships.

Community - Loyalty belongs to the community of family-first. Then expands outward to include the larger community to serve.

We Are All Human - Labels separate us. In our separation, we forget to see each other as human, with needs and desires. We see objects instead of people. When we forget to see each other as human, we fail to treat each other as human.

Acceptance - Life is accepted as it presents itself. There is no wasted time or energy wishing it was different. This conserves energy.

Proactive - The energy conserved from acceptance is used to proactively seek solutions by taking action.

Realistic - This characteristic removes any "rose-colored glasses" or "pain goggles" to address the "large pink elephants" in the room. Challenges are faced with courage. The faster a situation is realistically faced, the faster a solution can be found. (See Proactive, above.)

100-year Vision - Taking a 100-year vision means overlooking petty problems, putting relationships before being right, and seeing the big picture. Gerald and I considered selling our ranch in South Texas to become debt free, but when we took the 100-year view, we instantly realized that it was a gem to keep. Rather than take a shortcut to pay off debt, we would continue the payments we have made for the past decade.

As you proceed through the three phases of your Legacy Family Plan please keep the following 21 characteristics in mind. While several are similar, they are subtly different. Their combination is powerful and provides the foundation for a self-fulfilled life. When you accept 100% responsibility for your life, you don't feel victimized by life. You have the power to live your legacy.

Once "*IT*" is out, it's too late.

As you can see, Legacy Family Planning is different from traditional estate planning, because it focuses on the development of the family. It's easy to see why inheritances fail 85% of the time without a Legacy Family Plan in place. If you are concerned about how to incorporate all these new ideas into a plan, relax. The last half of this book is dedicated to guiding you through the process, one baby step at a time.

But if you're saying to yourself, "That won't happen to my family," or "I've already set up my estate plan, and I don't need more planning," I hate to be the bearer of bad news. You won't know that you are wrong until after "*IT*" happens. "IT" is the unleashing of the Cur$e of Inheritance. Once "*IT*" is out, it's too late.

And unfortunately, you just can't accurately predict how people will behave in an inheritance situation before it happens. You can, however, concentrate on building three strong pillars of lasting wealth. Without a Legacy Family Plan, you're gambling on your family's future, as well as your own.

Buddy's Story

Buddy is an old family friend of my parents. I've known his family for decades, and was shocked to hear his tale of horror when we connected a few years after his wife passed away. Buddy disappeared from Facebook following her death after a prolonged illness. Having buried his only daughter prior to his wife's death, his remaining family consisted of two granddaughters and their families. My inquiries to them did not receive a response. Honestly, I thought he had died too, and the girls were too grief-stricken to respond. When his wife passed, Buddy was 90-plus years old.

To say this family was close is an understatement. Buddy's granddaughters grew up in a house down the street with their single mom, in a home owned by their grandparents. This multi-generational family enjoyed dinners together most nights of the week. Buddy and his wife generously supported the girls and paid for vacations and college tuition, including medical school for one, and law school for the other. In all the time I spent with the family, I don't recall a harsh word spoken between them.

Imagine my surprise to receive an email from Buddy several years after his Facebook disappearance. Not only was he alive, he was still going strong! Since our re-connection, I have flown out to visit

Buddy several times. On our first visit, he shared the shocking and disturbing tale that explained why his granddaughters never responded to me. His story exemplifies how "IT" can destroy a family, and the danger of believing that it couldn't happen to you.

In the weeks following this wife's death, Buddy was forcibly removed from his own home at eight o'clock in the morning by staff from a mental hospital. It had been reported that Buddy was unable to care for himself and they were there to pick him up for an evaluation. In the week it took him to convince the hospital staff that HE WAS QUITE CAPABLE, his wife's jewelry and papers disappeared from the locked safe at home.

When his wife died, Buddy wasn't the executor of his wife's will. Years before, when he almost died, his wife changed her will and named their lawyer granddaughter as executrix. When Buddy fully recovered, the will was never updated. And really, given the loving family dynamics, why worry?

Why indeed? Since his release from the mental hospital, Buddy has spent years fighting his granddaughter for access to money he earned! Needless to say, relationships are ruined. He was able to evict her from the house she inhabited after her mother's death, and she moved as far away as the continent allows. It is a tragedy his great grandchildren won't have the opportunity to build a relationship with this World War II hero, and extraordinary kind and funny man.

What happened? Since I've only heard one side of the story, I can't say for sure. But what I do know is that if "IT" could happen to this close, loving family, it could happen to any family. Even yours.

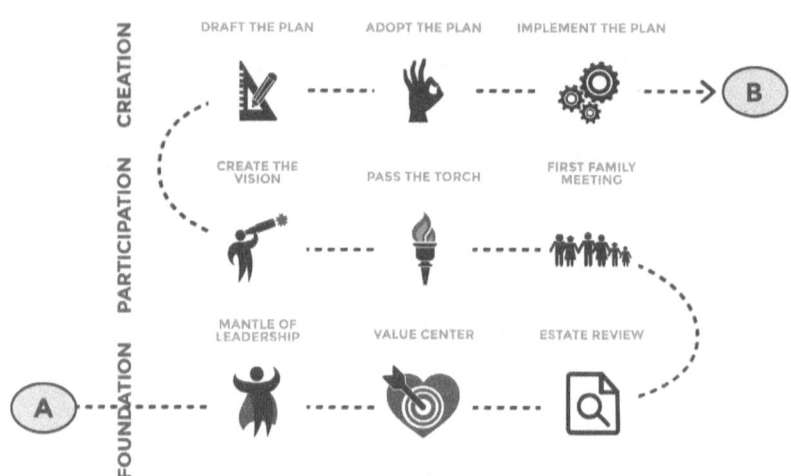

The Legacy Family Planning Process

Foundation Phase

Accept the Mantle of Leadership

Identify Core Value Center

Estate Plan Review

Participation Phase

First Family Meeting

Pass the Torch

Create the Vision

Creation Phase

Draft the Plan

Adopt the Plan

Implement the Plan

"The future belongs to those who give the next generation reason for hope."

—Pierre Teilhard De Chardin

Part One
Foundation Phase

"Real generosity toward the future lies in giving all to the present."

—Albert Camus

Chapter Four:
Accept the Mantle of Leadership

In this first phase, you will Accept the Mantle of Leadership, Identify Core Values and Complete an Estate Review. Everything you have learned so far has been preparing you for this moment. Building a solid foundation is the first phase of your Legacy Family Plan, and it begins by Accepting the Mantle of Leadership.

This first step requires you to make a choice before you take action. Not everyone is willing to accept the mantle of leadership. While I have fully embraced my role as the matriarch in my family, my husband Gerald is still struggling with this decision. It requires a consciousness mind-set, 100 years into the future viewpoint, and to live in truth. Doing so allows you to take the high road with family members. Something easier said than done. The good news is, it only takes one Family Founder to Accept the Mantle of Leadership to begin the process.

Accepting the mantle of leadership means you are now the matriarch or patriarch of your family. Not only are you a parent, or grandparent, in this expanded role you become the leader of your tribe. The foundation you are building now will provide for your family, both now and in the future. By tribe, I mean a community of people linked by common values and culture, with social and economic ties. Examples of family tribal leaders include Joseph

P. Kennedy, John W. Nordstrom, and Claes Maartenszen van Rosenvelt, the patriarch of the Roosevelt family.

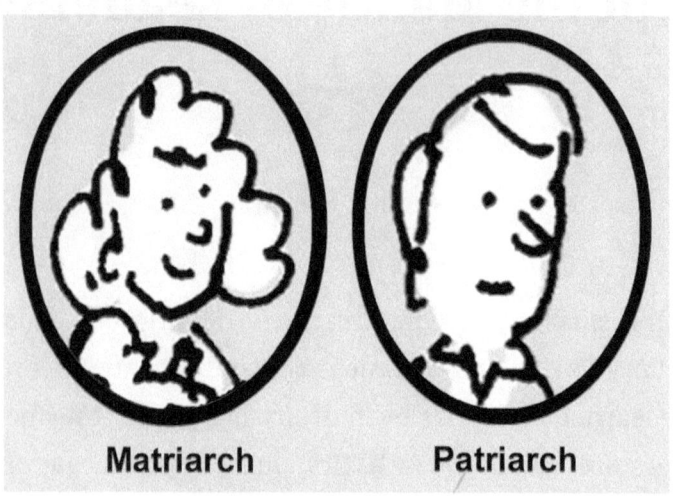

I believe we are spiritual beings living in a physical world. Walking 500 miles across Spain in 37 days with Ease and Grace allowed me to experience the power of consciousness mind-set. I'm not suggesting you need to follow in my footsteps, and although I don't want to get woo-woo, Spirituality is a key ingredient of Legacy Family Planning. Even if you don't believe in God/Universe/Spirit, please be open to the ideas presented. You don't have to understand how electricity gets from the power plant to your light fixture to enjoy its illumination. Consciousness mind-set is the same.

Looking 100 years into the future puts life into perspective. When my brother was wrongfully convicted of money laundering, his wife of thirty-plus years struggled to keep a roof over her head. Richard had always paid the bills and provided for his family. Rather than continuing to rent a tiny house that was falling apart, we helped Peggy purchase a small home she could earn equity on, and then became her mortgage company. We consider Peggy a part of our clan and invest in developing her skills. This is called "Capital Account Competencies," a concept covered in greater detail later in the book.

Living in truth opens the door for seeing life how it is, not how you wish it would be. When my brother, Richard, was convicted and went to prison, my sister-in-law found herself in financial straits. I couldn't look the other way and pretend everything was OK. I've accepted responsibility to support her while she gains the education and training she needs to become self-sufficient and 100% responsible for her life. We have had difficult conversations about her finances that would be easier to avoid. These conversations can be difficult, which is why accepting the mantle of leadership is so important.

After you make the decision to accept the mantle of leadership, it's time to take action and adopt a consciousness mind-set, look 100 years into the future and live in truth. The combined total of these three steps provides the mental foundation for your position as leader of your clan.

Consciousness Mind-set

A Millennial friend asked me about Legacy Families: "Do you need money to create a Legacy Family?" Mike is a successful entrepreneur who has escaped the gang-infested suburbs of Washington, D.C. where he was raised. His question hit home.

To provide him with an answer, I began researching poverty, the economic opposite of Legacy Families. In my search, I discovered

Ruby K. Payne, Ph.D. She is an authority on transitioning families out of poverty. In her book, I stumbled on her graph of poverty, middle class and wealth mind-sets. This allowed me to see the gap that exists between the wealthy mind-set and Legacy Family mind-set. The gap is consciousness mind-set.

Mindset Comparisons

Description	Poverty	Middle Class	Wealthy	Consciousness
Food	"Is there enough?"	"Does it taste good?"	"Was it presented well?"	"Is it nutritious?"
Money	To be used, spent	To be managed	To be conserved, invested	A resource to develop family members
Education	Valued, but not a reality	Crucial for climbing the ladder of success	Necessary tradition for making connections	Necessary for acquiring skills to become a master of life
Driving Focus	Survival, relationships, entertainment	Work, achievement	Financial, political, social connections	Development of unique gifts and talents to meet the world's needs

Adapted from: *A Framework for Understanding Poverty* by Ruby K. Payne, Ph.D.

What is consciousness? It is a difficult concept to nail down, and not my expertise to teach. Entire books on the subject by authors much more qualified than I are available if you are inspired to learn more about this fascinating topic. Merriam-Webster defines consciousness as:

- the condition of being conscious: the normal state of being awake and able to understand what is happening around you

- a person's mind and thoughts

- knowledge that is shared by a group of people

For me, consciousness has been a journey. Before my parents passed away, if someone had asked me about the body, mind and soul connection, I would have responded, "My body is a vehicle for my mind, and I own a soul." Based on my life experiences at the time, and the way I was raised, it reflected my beliefs. After my journey through "the dark night of the soul" my beliefs shifted. I now understand I am a soul, housed in a temporary body, and I recognize my mind as the Ego. I feel a connection to God and the world around me.

When you implement the 21 Key Characteristics from Chapter 3, you raise your consciousness. They provide a road map for valuing people over things, taking the high road, and seeing the consequences of our actions.

100-year Outlook

Accepting the mantle of leadership means adopting a 100-year outlook on life. Until there are radical breakthroughs in medicine, you will most likely not meet family members who will be born

100 years from now, which means they won't meet you either. However, when you keep this unborn generation in mind, you have the ability to become their hero. As the tribal leader you are laying the foundation for their future.

The decisions you make today matters. Your 100-year vision provides focus for daily activities and provides you with peace of mind. While others are agonizing over current events, you are calm. You see past the flavor-of-the-day madness to concentrate on taking action that is within your control. You have a sense of knowing that, this too shall pass.

An excellent example of this is the presidential election between Donald Trump and Hillary Clinton. I cast my vote and waited to see who won. I did my part by voting, but I had no control over the outcome. No matter who won, my job remained the same. As the nation convulsed in uproar, I began strategizing the best way to protect my family's future.

This strategy of protecting the family in the face of current events is one example of why Legacy Families are so successful. Their combined strength and commitment to each other enables them to navigate uncertain times with confidence. Rather than wasting energy on things beyond your control, concentrate on taking concrete steps to protect your family in changing environments.

On a more personal level, taking the 100-year view helps solve family challenges. It helps you focus on solutions instead of the problems. The way you resolve family issues today will affect relationships in the future. A broken relationship with a sibling multiplies. Cousins lose contact, and eventually, entire branches of the families become cut off.

Live in Truth

The last step in accepting the mantle of leadership requires you to live in truth. Legacy Family Leaders are quick to face tough situations. They don't ignore pink elephants in the room like drug addiction, domestic violence, or mental health issues, because they have the skills and confidence to solve them. They also have the financial resources to spend, as well as the propensity to see the expenditure as an investment in the family.

Legacy Families see life as their job and their family as a business. They use business tools to solve family challenges. SWOT analysis (Strengths, Weaknesses, Opportunities and Threats) allows the family to address issues that other families ignore. Like the weak link in a chain, the weakest relationship in the family determines the family's strength. Your family is only as strong as its weakest member, and its weakest relationship. Strengthen the weaknesses of your weakest family member, and you strengthen the entire family. Investing in this relationship is one of the highest priorities of the Legacy Family Plan.

"Decisions are easy when your values are clear."

—Roy Disney

Chapter Five:
Identify Your Value Center

Now that you have accepted the mantle of leadership, you are ready to complete the second step in the process: Identify Your Value Center. In this step you will create a draft version of your top 5 values, Capital Account Competency List, family mission and vision statements, inspiring family story and mantra. Understand that this is a draft only.

In the next phase you will ask your Rising Generation to participate by identifying their value center and then come together to create a shared vision. In the third phase, this shared value center and vision will form the foundation for your Legacy Family Plan. They are the generation that will be responsible for bringing your Legacy Family Plan to life, so it only makes sense to ask them to participate in its creation.

Why take the time to go through this step now, only to repeat it again with your rising generation? Rather than ask a larger group to create from scratch, input is limited to you and your significant other, which is infinitely easier to accomplish. When you invite your family's input, they will be in edit mode, not creation mode, which is better suited to a large group. In addition, the time between the two sessions allows ideas, stories and ideas to percolate that invariably improve the plan.

For your DIY plan, I recommend you take the same approach we use in our workshops and retreats. In your more relaxed home atmosphere, you can probably get this step done in a few hours by setting aside a half day, or spread out over several evenings. Make this a special event, however that looks like to you. What you are creating is incredibly special. You are laying the foundation for your family's future for the next 100 years! If you enjoy wine, pour a glass of your favorite. If you have the time, get away from your daily routine and spend a few days in your most comfortable environment, be it beach, mountain, or desert.

Make your binder. I recommend you use a 3-inch, 3-ring binder with section dividers to organize your documents. If you enjoy being creative, purchase a binder with a clear slip and decorate a front cover for your book. Have fun with this. If you travel, be sure to bring your binder with you. Prior to this DIY Step 2, download and print the *Step 2 Download Documents* at www.LegacyFamilyRevolution.com/LFWdownload.

I find it's very powerful to begin your session by connecting with God/Source/Universe. Say a prayer, light a candle, diffuse essential oils, meditate, or any other practice that invites God/Universe/Source into your process. Ask for guidance. This is a rewarding journey, not just for your family's future, but for you and your spouse. No matter how long you have known each other, this process will draw you together in a deeper way. And if you are single, the journey is equally rewarding. You will discover inner truths that may be surprising.

Begin by completing the value exercise to determine your top 5 values. Creating a value-centered estate plan is liberating, because it provides a touchstone to make decisions with your time and money. Your top-five values are the core of your Legacy Family Plan. In time, these core values will direct all your other estate planning tools. Ultra-high-net families use their value center to guide their investment decisions, making it easier to evaluate potential deals. Advisors welcome the direction this provides because it saves time for everyone. This also directs how resources are invested to develop family members' mastery of skills listed in the Capital Account Competency List.

Identify Your Top 5 Values

Plan on spending half an hour for this exercise alone. I suggest you and your partner do this exercise at the same time, in separate locations, so that you can complete the exercise on your own. If this is not a possibility, just respect each other's privacy. Find a quiet place, without distraction. Have several sheets of paper, this book, the *Step 2 Download Documents* and your favorite pen. Spend a few minutes in quiet meditation, then review the Core Values List. As you read the values, place a dot next to any value that speaks to you. Check as many as you like as you go through the list. Once you are done, transfer the values you checked onto the next sheet. Now, read the list of favorites you created and circle your top 10 choices. Keep this original list, you will refer to those values later when you meet with your co-founder, and again when you meet with your family. Create a new list of your top 10 values. Save these lists in your binder.

It's time to reconnect with your partner to narrow each of your top ten values to a combined list of top five values. Any values you both share go on the top 5 list. Any remaining slots will be a negotiation between you. When you review your original lists, are there any values that are shared by both of you? The method you use to come to an agreement doesn't matter as long as it represents your combined core values. Be aware that this list might change when you invite your children into the process. For now, the list should represent you and your co-founder.

Congratulations on completing the Top 5 Values exercise! Now, it's time to create your Capital Account Competency List.

In your *Step 2 Download* packet, I included a draft of the Capital Account Competency List that Gerald and I created for our family's consideration. Please, use what resonates, add items we missed and ignore the rest.

Keep your initial list short, 3 to 5 items per capital account, at most. Don't make the same mistake Gerald and I did and overwhelm your family. Make room for them to add to the list instead of wanting to erase skills you know are important.

Your Capital Account Competency List will become your guide for developing skills for yourself and your family members. One of the benefits of Legacy Family Planning is that you can learn right alongside your family; you don't have to be the expert in everything. In each of the categories, I encourage you to consider how you will pass this training program from one generation to the next while adapting to constant change.

Human Capital Account Competencies

Your top 5 values may be the core of your Family Plan, but the Human Capital Account Competencies are the heart and soul that make everything else work. Authenticity, balanced living, communication, emotional intelligence, healthy boundaries, vulnerability, gratitude, values and empathy are a sampling of human capital skills. Human Capital competency training is a lifelong development, learning program at the family level. The Human Capital Competency List was the longest and most robust list that Gerald and I created. What human capital competencies do you believe are necessary to live a life of prosperity, joy and fulfillment? Create your draft list and do your best to limit the list to no more than 5 skills.

Intellectual Capital Account Competencies

In business, intellectual capital is an asset that is broadly defined as the collection of all informational resources a company owns for its business. According to a Merrill Lynch article titled "Creating Meaning from Money," intellectual capital is the *"The principles, policies, practices in a family that create structure to develop a shared vision of family money and sense of accountability that influences the actions and decisions family members make every day."*

Gerald and I created a basic competency list for our family to help family members determine their learning styles, and create a lifelong, learning goal. We both value education, but realize not everyone is college material. Our competency list provides for alternative forms of education, as well as formal education. What intellectual capital account competencies do you believe are necessary to live a life of prosperity, joy and fulfillment? Create your draft list and do your best to limit the list to no more than 5 skills.

Social Capital Account Competencies

When Gerald and I moved to Boerne, I didn't know anyone except our real estate agent. Before the move, I prayed my skills and talents would be used to help my new community. Within months of the move, I was volunteering on a gala committee to raise funds to build a women's shelter. It was a good fit for me because my youngest daughter escaped an abusive relationship in college. My volunteering efforts resulted in my becoming the President of the Board of Directors, and for a short time, I was the paid Executive Director. From my efforts, I learned the non-profit industry from the inside, and how to evaluate the effectiveness of a non-profit organization. It's not what you think; the 80/20 rule is out of date. That is why the Social Competency List Gerald and I created asks the question: "How will you measure success for your contribution?" Do you know how to effectively measure a non-profit's contribution? If not, get educated so that you can obtain the highest return on your donation of time, talent and treasure. What Social Capital Account Competencies do you believe are necessary to live a life of prosperity, joy and fulfillment? Create your draft list and do your best to limit the list to no more than 5 skills.

Financial Capital Account Competencies

The Merrill Lynch definition for the Financial Capital account is "the meaning *created from money when used to grow other capital sources and fulfill one's own purpose and potential. It is a means to an end, but not the end goal.*" This helped me see the Financial Capital account in a new way, because it easily explains that wealth's importance comes from the meaning that is attached to it, instead of a number on the bottom of a financial report.

For this capital account, the list Gerald and I created was both practical and spiritual in nature. Its focus is on a healthy relationship with money, prosperity, lifestyle and stewardship. We have benefited from completing Julia Cameron's *The Prosperous Heart* as well as Dave Ramsey's *Financial Peace University*. What Financial Capital Account Competencies do you believe are necessary to live a life of prosperity, joy and fulfillment? Create your draft list and do your best to limit the list to no more than 5 skills.

You have now identified your top 5 values and 12 to 20 essential skills for your Capital Account Competency List. Now it's time to write a draft mission and vision statement. Make this a fun and easy process. Create statements with meaning. Typically, simple and easy to remember is better than a bunch of meaningless words.

> *"A family mission statement is a combined, unified expression from all family members of what your family is all about – what it is you really want to do and be – and the principles you choose to govern your family life."*
> —**Stephen Covey**

Mission Statement

Creating a family mission statement gives your family members a sense of belonging. It puts into words the standards of behavior that all members agree to uphold. Ideally, it is easy to remember.

Vision Statement

When you look 100 years into the future, what do you see? What is your vision of success for your family? Creating a vision statement bonds each rising generation to a sense of values and purpose and provides a feeling of being part of something special.

Family Story and Mantra

You have almost finished! Human beings relate to stories. Every family has a wealth of stories. You just have to find one that highlights a principle or value that you admire. It must be a story with a hero's arc. Someone had to overcome a hardship. The hero can be anyone, even a dog! Once you select your story, it's time to create an easy-to-remember, catchy phrase, or mantra. Stories are infinitely more powerful in binding your family together. Unlike a mission statement or vision statement, stories are easy to remember.

An excellent example of a unifying family story comes from an article I read years ago in a *Cowboys and Indians* magazine. The article was written about a family-owned business that I admired. Even though it's been years, I remember it because of my interest in family legacies and storytelling. This is the power of a story. The Double D Ranch company sells beautiful women's western wear and is owned and operated by the McMullen family.

According to the article, the family faced tough times with a rally cry of "Red's got it." This phrase reminded the family to be tenacious in the pursuit of their dreams. The story originated from the founder's childhood. While walking his dog, Red, across dusty trails, he would flush rabbits from the brush. "Red always caught his rabbit. And now, three generations of business owners encourage themselves and each other with a simple phrase, "Red's got it." Like an inside joke that binds people together, your family mantra is inspiring and makes family members feel special, something bigger than themselves.

What value or values are important to you? What hero's story highlights this value? What phrase will inspire your family?

Congratulations on completing the second step of the Foundation Level of your Legacy Family Plan. The values you identified will positively impact your family for generations to come. They will guide you, your family and your advisors on the investment of your financial assets. The Capital Account Competency List you created provides a lifelong learning program for the self-development of your family members. This gives them the skills they need to live up to the family mission and vision. And the unifying story creates a culture of belonging.

> *"The best time to plant a tree was 20 years ago.*
>
> *The second best time is now."*
>
> **—Chinese Proverb**

Chapter Six: Estate Review

Congratulations, you are almost done with the Foundation Phase of your Legacy Family Plan. In this final step of the first phase you will review your estate. Traditionally, when you hear estate review, you think of legal documents and your financial assets. And, you are correct, you will review these two traditional aspects of wealth. But they are only a part of the review you will complete for this step. As I've stated before, the traditional approach to wealth transfer isn't enough to create lasting wealth. Rather than limiting your estate review to legal documentation and financial assets, you will also review your ability to face the topic of death in your quest to become an Anticipator, and review your family relationships to prepare for your Legacy Family Plan.

Asset and Legal Documentation Review

Your meetings with your advisors will serve a dual purpose. You will be obtaining information from them about the status of your estate, and assessing your advisor's skills to meet your future needs. This is a good time to picture how they will interact with your family, after you are gone. Do they have the personality, character, knowledge and heart to serve your family's highest good? You don't have to answer this question now, just observe. In the third phase, you will be building a Board of Directors (BOD). Is your current advisor the right fit for your board?

Begin your estate review by meeting with your wealth advisor(s) and CPA. You are on a fact-finding mission. What is the current value of your financial assets? Are all the beneficiaries up to date? Are bank accounts correct? How do tax law changes affect your estate plan? Based on the economy, your lifestyle, health and your age, do you have adequate assets to live in comfort to the end?

Check, and double check, **all your asset titles**. Review everything that requires legal documentation to transfer ownership: automobiles, real estate, including oddballs, like horses and livestock. Imagine the shock of learning that your husband's or wife's life insurance proceeds will be going to his ex-wife or her ex-husband. Over and over again I hear financial planners say, "I begged my client to check all his polices. We updated the ones under my management, but he didn't follow up with his other advisors." Take control of your financial future by examining all aspects of your financial assets with your advisors.

How long has it been since you updated your estate plan? For most folks, this task gets lost in the cracks of daily life. What's changed since your last review? Is your estate plan congruent with your values? Is it time for an update?

Although Bobby Kennedy was the Attorney General for the United States, he didn't update his will after his brother, John F. Kennedy, was killed in 1963. Five years later, on June 6, 1968, when Sirhan Sirhan shot and killed Bobby, his will still listed his late brother as his executor.

Failure to update your will is the second greatest estate planning mistake behind not having one. Meet with your legal advisors and review the legal documents that will determine the distribution of your estate.

In the blink of an eye, your ability to change your estate plan can disappear. Having a stroke, accident, disease can affect your ability to plan for your future. NOW is the time to review and make any necessary updates. After Mom was diagnosed with Alzheimer's, her will could no longer be changed. When Dad changed his will, their estate plans were no longer compatible, which resulted in time, heartache and enormous attorney fees to resolve.

Do you have enough?

Where are you on your lifestyle? Are you ready to downsize, or are you looking to add a second vacation home? Do you have enough? This is an important question to answer. Will you know when you have enough?

Towards the end of my parents' lives, they were generating excess income each month from their portfolio of commercial properties. They enjoyed their 9th hole golf course view and swimming pool, a motorhome to roam the countryside, comfortable automobiles and no debt. They had everything they ever wanted, and then some. More than once, Dad asked me what to do with the money. Every time, my answer was the same: "Spend it on your family." And every time, his response was the same: "Spending it on the family doesn't make me money."

He couldn't have been more wrong. In the decade following his death, many of the assets he worked so hard to accumulate are gone. Looking back, I see how right my instincts were. Had I known about Legacy Families at the time, I could have shared my research and proven to him the benefits of investing in family. And, I'd like to believe he would have listened.

How about you? Do you have enough? Or, do you have more than enough to begin investing in your family? Based on my research, it is the best investment you can make. Do you see the benefits of investing in family?

Stewardship Plan

Whether you have enough or more than enough, it's time to create a Stewardship Plan. What is a Stewardship Plan and why should you have one? In the non-profit world, the stewardship plan shows donors that funds entrusted to the organization's care were invested wisely. It is a communication tool of accountability and gratitude.

At the family level, the Stewardship Plan provides guidance for investing financial resources. Based on the values, mission and vision you defined in the previous chapter, your Stewardship Plan helps create a culture of shared resources instead of individual ownership. It encourages growth instead of consumption. It transforms spending into investing. Expenditures are measured as an exchange of value and expands money consciousness.

When you take time to ask yourself, "Is this an investment I value?" as you hand over the cash, check or credit card, you increase your awareness of spending patterns. Carry a small notebook in your pocket and track every penny you spend. Use one page per day, and each time you spend, write down in your notebook (1.) who you paid (2.) how much you spent and (3.) "yes" or "no." "Yes" means you invested in your life according to your values. "No" means you didn't. Following this practice, it won't take long for patterns to emerge.

Recognizing the pattern makes it easier to make a different choice in the future. "Ah, here it is again." The discipline of writing down every penny makes us accountable to ourselves. Faced with the prospect of writing down $4.87 for a coke and candy, I pass. And in this state of awareness and choice, I am congruent with my pocketbook and values.

On a larger scale, your stewardship plan serves as a guide for the highest and best use of your financial assets, based on your values. How much do you invest in social capital? How do you evaluate the result of your contribution? And when you have more than enough, how do you invest the excess funds? Do you give up control of some assets? Do you invest in the education and development of your children and grandchildren? Why not invest in your family's success now? Don't make them wait until you're dead to invest in their success, especially if you have more than enough now.

To be clear, I am not talking about lifestyle enhancing gifts, I'm talking about skills you determine are important to develop from your Capital Account Competency List.

Become an Anticipator

"Picture it. You are alone in a white room with nice even light. There are no windows, no doors, and no way out. How do you feel?" Stop. For just a moment, consider how you are feeling. Please don't read further until you answer the question. How are you feeling about being in the room?

Back in the 1990s, I ran across a psychology test, and this was one of the questions. I enjoyed asking this question, along with the others from the test, because the responses were fascinating. Dad's response was ballistic: "You can't keep me in there, I'll find a way out." My now ex-husband was the complete opposite: "I'll enjoy my time alone."

How did you respond? According to the creators of the test, your response to this question reflects your feelings about death. Are you comfortable in the room, or do you want out? Based on the responses I received from my surveys, it is accurate in determining levels of comfort concerning death. Is it accurate for you?

Getting comfortable with death is one of the secrets to creating lasting wealth. See life through your heirs' eyes. How would your absence affect them? I'm not talking about the grieving process; I'm talking about the relationships between your heirs and their ability to thrive without you. How will they behave towards one another in regards to their inheritance from your estate? How will they carry the family culture forward after you are gone? Will they stay unified and continue your legacy, or will they splinter apart, and reduce the family fortune? Do they have self-esteem, self-confidence and passion?

SWOT Analysis

SWOT is an acronym for Strengths, Weaknesses, Opportunities and Threats. The ability to successfully transfer wealth is directly tied to the health of your family relationships. Your family is only as strong as its weakest relationship. Relying on legal documents to create lasting wealth just doesn't work, because it doesn't address the real issue which is the relationships between family members. To be successful, your family needs to see itself as a single unit. Your SWOT analysis provides you with actionable steps to strengthen your family relationships.

SWOT analysis was created for business application in the 1960s, but it is equally effective for the Legacy Family Planning process. This is for your eyes only. It is an analytical tool for the Family Founders to logically look at their family, relationships, financial assets, and begin to anticipate how to prepare their family to thrive in their absence.

The purpose of conducting a SWOT analysis at this point in the Legacy Family Planning process is to identify the factors affecting your family's future and create a draft plan to address them. Strengths and weaknesses are internal factors. Opportunities and threats are external factors. Strategies are focused on leveraging strengths and opportunities and overcoming weaknesses and threats to fulfill the family mission and vision.

This is not the time to deny or ignore any issues. If you have a child with an addiction problem, write it down. If your business is at risk, write it down. Be courageous in identifying all the factors in the weaknesses and threats quadrants.

Allow ideas to bubble forth without filtering. Be equally real in identifying strengths and opportunities; now is not the time for modesty. Spend 30 to 45 minutes identifying as many factors for each quadrant as you can.

STRENGTHS	WEAKNESSES
OPPORTUNITIES	THREATS

With all the factors identified, it's time to rank them into three categories. I prefer A, B and C, or 1, 2, and 3. Rank each factor in one quadrant before moving on to the next.

With each item ranked, it's time to identify recommendations and strategies to leverage strengths and opportunities and overcome weaknesses and threats. Focus on one or two items only and create a SMART strategy for achieving your goal. SMART stands for Specific, Measurable, Achievable, Realistic and Time-based.

When Gerald and I conducted our first SWOT analysis, we identified the debt we incurred to settle my parents' estate as a weakness, and our nation's debt policy as a threat to our family's future. We identified our real estate and business acumen as our opportunity and strengths to overcome our weakness. Our SMART goal is to eliminate our debt by December 31, 2017.

Foundation Phase Review

You have made tremendous progress, congratulations! You have completed the Foundation Phase of your Legacy Family Plan and are now ready to move into the next phase, the Participation Phase. In preparation, you have Accepted the Mantle of Leadership, Identified your Value Center and completed an Estate Review.

You began the journey by adopting a consciousness mind-set, taking a 100-year view, and living in truth. You named your top 5 values, created a Capital Account Competency List, drafted your Family Mission and Vision Statements, and found a heroic family story and mantra. As you reviewed your financial assets and legal documents, you observed and assessed your advisors. You answered tough questions, "Do I have enough?" and "How do I feel about death?" You created a Stewardship Plan, conducted a SWOT analysis and created SMART goals.

You now have a better understanding of who you are, what you value, the status of your estate and a plan to move forward. With this information, you are now ready to introduce Legacy Family Planning to your rising generation, and invite them to join you on the journey. You will ask them to accept the torch, to become the next generation of leaders, and co-create a shared vision for the future.

"Every family has a story. Only a few have a legacy."
—Carrie L. Huntley

Part Two
Participation Phase

"Let us learn to skillfully draw good out of what would otherwise cause us harm."

—St. Mary Euphrasia Pelletier

Chapter Seven: First Family Meeting

In the first phase of this process, you discovered internal wisdom and sought input from your advisors. Now, it's time to ask your heirs to have conversations about incredibly personal and volatile topics. Together, you will explore answers to some difficult questions. Don't be surprised if you share both laughter and tears along the way.

Based on the status of your current relationships identified in your SWOT analysis, it's time to ask yourself an important question. Is it in your family's highest and best interest to proceed on your own, or is now the time to hire a Legacy Family Planner?

Had Mom and Dad attempted to lead our family through this phase of the Legacy Family Plan, I am confident it would have been a disaster. Between Dad's need for control, inability to empathize and lack of listening skills, I can easily see this first meeting turning into a shouting match with people running for the exit. We were a competitive dysfunctional family with underlying and unresolved issues.

But even if the above scenario had played out, it would have been a worthwhile effort. The underlying issues would have been exposed while my parents were alive. There was a missed opportunity to resolve them, or at least reach a family-wide acknowledgment of the permanent break. Honestly, I am quite certain my parents would not have attempted to lead this process on their own. Dad believed in hiring help in areas outside of his expertise, and my parents were well aware of the problems that existed in our family.

Sadly, some relationships can't be fixed. Unfortunately, for a multitude of reasons, estranged family members are not uncommon. This situation does not prevent families from creating a Legacy Family Plan, rather, it increases the need for one. Broken relationships may exist between two people, or the estrangement may include the entire family.

Hopefully you heeded my recommendation to read the book in its entirety before beginning the process. If you followed my recommendation and decided to hire a Legacy Family Planner, then you have a base knowledge and know what to expect. If, after reading the book, you are committed to a DIY process, you know what's coming and can craft a meaningful invitation for your family. Don't rush into this first family meeting. Take your time to prepare for it.

What can you expect?

My best advice: don't set expectations. Instead, remain focused on your desired outcome. Expectations are funny; they show up in surprising places and at the least expected times. Walking the Camino de Santiago helped me discover that my life was full of expectations I wasn't aware of setting. When I found myself disappointed with an experience, I discovered it was usually because I had created an expectation and didn't know it. Walking 500 miles across Spain taught me to identify what was really happening and shift my focus to my desired outcome.

After trudging the steep climb to the top of the hill of forgiveness, I was upset to see a food truck marring the landscape. This was one of the iconic scenes from the movie, *The Way*. I didn't see a food truck while watching the movie! The depth of my feelings surprised me. A quick internal scan helped me recognize my discontent was the effect of unmet expectations. Once I discovered the source of my upset, I was able to put the feelings aside, shift my focus and continue my journey with a renewed sense of peace.

As you go through this process, if you find yourself upset and don't know why, ask yourself if you have an expectation that you weren't aware of, that isn't being met.

The Purpose of the First Family Meeting Step

The name of this step of the process is First Family Meeting, which is a little misleading. Depending on your family, you may be able to complete this step in a single meeting, or you may need to host a series of meetings before family members are willing to make a decision. The purpose of this step is to receive an answer to one important question: Is your family willing to participate in co-creating a Legacy Family Plan?

To clarify, this step will last as long as it takes for your family to reach a decision. Either they are willing to participate and eventually accept the torch of leadership, or they aren't. What happens if some family members are willing to participate, and others are not? This is one of the most difficult decisions you will face during this process. How will you face this situation if it arises? Discuss your options now and be prepared.

During this step you will provide your family with the information they need to make an educated decision. They won't be able to answer unless they have information about the process. What is your desired goal? What's in it for them? And why should they participate? Answer these questions for yourself in preparation of your invitation to your family.

Dad wanted to create a real estate empire. Not only did he want to provide income to make life easier for his children and grandchildren, it made him feel good about himself. He worked his way out of poverty during the Depression and unfortunately, his self-esteem was tied to his financial accomplishment. Legacy Family Planning was unknown to him and he relied on legal documents, which resulted in the destruction of our family and failure to achieve his goal for his family.

What is your goal, and why do you want this? Carefully articulate your *why* and desired outcome so that your family will want to attend. This is a critical component of your invitation.

The Invitation

Who will you invite to your first family meeting? Depending on your family dynamics, would it be beneficial to conduct an initial meeting with your children only, then have another meeting with in-laws, children and other family members? If your children are married, is their marriage stable? Will you invite their spouses? If you jointly own a business with relatives (siblings, cousins, etc.), what about their families? What about young children? How old does a child need to be to attend the meeting? Who are the beneficiaries of your will?

As long as your family likes each other and you don't expect fireworks, inviting young children who can sit quietly without disrupting the meeting is a good idea. Imagine the impact on this child, and their ability to bridge your legacy to future generations! When they become a grandparent, they can hold a grandchild on their lap and share their firsthand EXPERIENCE of attending the first family meeting.

Gerald and I brought our six-year-old grandson, Christian, to a meeting with our attorney and CPA. After we completed our estate review, we realized we needed to update our wills. We also invited our oldest daughter, Tiffany, to come with us. We wanted her to hear the discussion, and begin fostering a relationship with our advisors. Tiffany is our office manager, executrix and mother to two girls under the age of three.

Christian's attendance at the meeting came from an emergency request from our youngest daughter, Brittany. It was the summer, and he was out of school. Brittany is a kindergarten teacher and had just been notified of mandatory district training, and her police officer husband was unable to change his schedule to help.

Although Christian's attendance wasn't planned, his presence was welcome. He is a budding artist, happy to quietly create his artwork when provided with a pen and blank paper. Gerald and I were excited for the unexpected opportunity to introduce him to estate planning. I was curious to see what he would get out of the meeting. In the conference room, Christian quietly drew during the entire meeting and never said a word. On the ride home, I asked him, "What did you learn today?" His response was astonishing. "Elmo, it's not a good idea to give people too much money at one time." I was stunned by the wisdom and understanding. It's so simple, even a six-year-old understands.

Before you send out your invitations, take a moment to reflect on how it will be received by each invitee. Find a quiet place to reflect. Bring your binder, pen and paper. On a sheet of paper, write down the names of everyone you are inviting to the meeting. After making the list, pause and reflect on each name, one at a time. See your invitation through their eyes. Are they excited? Scared? Nervous? Confused? Worried? Angry? How do they feel to receive an invitation to a family meeting? Take the time to connect with them. Jot down your response next to their name, and continue the process for each attendee. Be sure to include your partner. This exercise helps you understand how your family members may be feeling about the meeting so that you can be sensitive to their needs.

The Meeting

Prepare for your meeting, or meetings, with care. Now that you know who you are inviting, and have seen the invitation through their eyes, do you have confidence your family can complete this step in one meeting, or would it be best to conduct a series of meetings? When is the best time to schedule your first meeting? Weekend or weekday? Where will the meeting be held? Do you want to prepare handouts? Are you inviting your advisors? How long will the meeting last? Is there time for a family meal afterwards? Does it involve travel for some family members? Who will pay those expenses? What if someone can't attend, will you still have the meeting? Obviously, there are many details to consider.

After Gerald and I completed our Foundation Phase, we made the decision to introduce our daughters and their husbands to this idea by hosting a series of meetings. It had been eight years since our last family seminar, so we started with a mini-seminar at the attorney's office. We invited our sons-in-law, but no grandchildren since they are all under the age of six. Unfortunately, one of our daughters had a last-minute work conflict and could not attend. We have one daughter in Austin and two in the Dallas area, so scheduling around travel and work schedules was challenging. Our attorney provided an overview of our estate plan and answered technical questions. The remaining portion of the 90-minute meeting was led by Gerald and me, where we discussed legacy versus inheritance. That night, we had a family meal and enjoyed each other's company. If distance is a problem for your family, consider using technology, such as video conferencing with Skype or Zoom, to include them in the process.

The next family meeting was held months later at the "beach house" in McKinney. This house is across the street from my daughter, Tiffany. It serves as our office and provides me with a place to stay when I am in town. It is an excellent location for family meetings and get-togethers. In this second meeting, we asked the question, "Are you willing to participate in this process and eventually accept the torch of leadership?" Their response was, "We need more information and want to spend more time together, without you or Gerald."

The third time we met, the girls and their husbands participated in a fun team-building exercise, an "escape room," and enjoyed a meal together afterwards. Following their adventure, they reconvened at the house. At this meeting, they agreed to participate in the process, and we were able to move on to the next step of passing the torch.

Ground Rules

It is important to establish ground rules for your Legacy Family Meetings. These are not therapy sessions. They are family *business* meetings and everyone's conduct should match the occasion. Imagine you work in a large corporation, and you are invited to attend the managing directors' strategy session. How will you act and communicate? At a minimum, you will:

- Wait your turn to speak
- Really listen to other people's ideas and suspend judgment
- Be respectful
- Come prepared
- Be on time
- Share your best ideas
- Ask clarifying questions
- Seek the highest good for the organization

Ground rules aside, emotions are bound to bubble to the surface.

In our second meeting, we had several emotional moments. Unexpressed hurts were released, some childhood resentments surfaced, as well as a few "stories." We tell ourselves stories about our life that may or may not be based in truth. They are based on beliefs that we may not even know we have, like "You always treat me different." These beliefs color what we see.

Have you ever thought about buying a new car, and then suddenly start seeing it everywhere? Before I purchased my first Lincoln MKX, I never saw one on the road. But afterward, I started seeing them everywhere. Our stories are similar. When we have a belief, we look for evidence to support our story. Even if we have to overlook 9 instances where we were treated the same, we latch on to the one time we were treated different.

It was a bit awkward during these emotional moments. But awkward can be good when it results in shared feelings and starts the healing process.

With your family onboard, it's time to pass the torch of leadership.

"Life is a very narrow bridge between two eternities.

Be not afraid."

—Rabbi Nachman of Braslav

Chapter Eight: Pass the Torch

Passing the torch of leadership takes time. The previous step required resolution before you could move on. This second step in the second phase of Participation is the opposite. It never ends. The purpose of this step is to train your heirs to receive their inheritance, and this is a lifelong process. You will be training them to care for financial assets, working with advisors, as well as providing personal development training.

Financial Assets

Your asset mix will determine your training program. According to my daughter, my ex-husband's estate plan can be summed up on a single piece of paper. She knows, because he showed her. It was her training program. On the sheet, he listed his investment accounts, properties and business. At the bottom of the page, he included potential buyers of the non-liquid assets in case the girls want to sell them. It is simple, clean and will be easy for them to settle. Although his plan is simple, his net worth is impressive.

Because my parents created an elaborate estate plan with family limited partnerships and trusts, my estate plan is more complicated. And, to add fuel to the fire, I have started several businesses in the past few years. It takes a flow chart with arrows to track the ownership shares of my business assets, which means it will take longer to train the next generation.

Training Program

When my father contracted pneumonia in the midst of lung cancer treatment, he spent a week in the hospital. He was still optimistic about beating the disease, and during my visits we reminisced, laughed and shared many meaningful conversations. He bragged how buying me a horse at thirteen taught me work ethics. How he endured ten years of "I want a horse" harassment from me, I'll never know. But in that hospital room, he shared his deliberate plan of waiting until I was old enough to work so I could pay for the horse myself.

In five years, he promoted me from being Mom's assistant bookkeeper for the wholesale automobile company to president of the trucking company. By the time I was 18, I was responsible for keeping three car haulers legal in 21 states, and could transfer automobile titles, detail a car and close out the books each month on ledger sheets (this was before computers). I'll always remember the Friday morning I arrived at work to discover I was flying to Miami, Florida with a $500,000 cashier's check and instructions to double check the titles. He brilliantly used my passion for horses to give me business experiences that only entrepreneur families can provide.

It takes time to transfer knowledge from one generation to another. When Tiffany joined our commercial real estate company, I realized it would take years to train her. She has received her real estate license, and is working on obtaining her broker's license. In Texas, this is a four to five-year process. If I die before she is eligible to become a broker, our family will have to hire a broker to manage our business or shut it down.

I love entrepreneurship and the lifestyle it provides. My new businesses are based on progressive ownership models, similar to New Belgium Brewery in Fort Collins, Colorado. Positions will be filled with passionate team players who are using their strengths. And, yes, I believe in nepotism.

The Family Business

If you have a family business, I highly suggest you read two impactful novels by Tom Deans, Ph.D. *Every Family's Business* and *Willing Wisdom*. These books changed my beliefs about transferring businesses from one generation to the next. They were among the first in my research and introduced me to an entire new way of thinking about our commercial real estate business. If the rising generation doesn't have a passion for the business, it may be better to sell the business at the height of its value, instead of expecting the next generation to keep it afloat. Lack of passion will eventually kill a business. This is a factor in the shirtsleeves-to-shirtsleeves cycle of wealth transfer loss.

On the other hand, if one member of the family does have a passion for the business that is not shared by others, it makes sense to sell the business to the working family member to prevent future problems. My favorite pizza is but a distant memory because two brothers inherited equal halves of the business after their mom passed away. The non-working brother demanded "his half of the profit" without setting foot in the restaurant. Meanwhile, his brother was putting in 70-hour weeks. Rather than fighting a losing battle, Mark closed the business forever, leaving raving fans of their 54-year-old establishment longing for one more bite of childhood comfort food. So, sometimes selling the family business is the best option.

Board of Directors

Now is a good time to create a Board of Directors for your family and host an introductory meeting. In addition to your CPA, attorney and wealth managers, I suggest adding a mentor or coach. The most successful people I know are supported by a personal coach. The most successful families I know are supported by a mentor. Our board of directors also includes our banker. We can trace our family's relationship to this family-owned bank back to the 1800s. My great-grandfather took out a loan on his life insurance. We know this because when the bank cleaned out their vault in December 1999, they found the collateral for his loan and returned it to us.

Who will you include on your board? Contact your advisors, tell them about your Legacy Family Plan. Interview them. Are they the right advisor for your family? We replaced one of our advisors, and after twenty years of service, it was very difficult. Unfortunately, he couldn't see my vision for our family's future, so it was the right thing for our family to find a replacement. Since Tiffany is our executrix, she was involved in finding a replacement and has become the contact person for our family. We are building a multi-generational relationship which will serve our family's needs well into the future.

Create a Legacy Drawer

Dave Ramsey, famous for his Financial Peace Academy, recommends creating a legacy drawer. A single location of information your family will need to settle your estate. Make it easy for them. Tell your children where to find the documents. Our drawer is a fireproof, locked filing cabinet.

Write a draft obituary; you'll be glad you did. Write it as a work of fiction, put all your dreams and goals into it "as if" they were done. Doing so helps you discover what is really important in life and how you want to be remembered. I update my draft obituary every year on New Year's Eve. Since starting this yearly practice, I am more motivated, act congruently with how I want to be remembered, and I am appreciative of each day above ground.

Share Important Information

When you share important information with your heirs, it's important to do it at one time, with everyone in the room. If someone can't be there, you may decide to postpone the conversation, or if it is an option, have a spouse attend for them. Videotaping or recording the meeting is another excellent option. Provide an agenda of the meeting with a summary of the discussion for future reference.

We shared the outline of our estate plan with our family. They know Tiffany is our executrix and backup medical power of attorney. We have discussed our wishes for end-of-life care, and they have a copy of our asset ownership flow chart. We have pre-paid our cremation, and our urns are in our closet. By preparing them now, before a crisis occurs, we are empowering them with the knowledge, confidence and tools to help us age with dignity and grace.

Stuff

When Gerald's mother passed away, we found food in the freezer that was over ten years old. When my parents passed away, we threw medicine away that had expired decades before. In the garage, we found one of Dad's snorkel flippers. I have no idea why he kept one flipper. Maybe he thought the other one would show up one day? I'm sure growing up during the Depression made it difficult for him to throw anything away. But, my most challenging find was his penis pumps. Yep, not one, but two. He was a prostate cancer survivor and I guess he had one for the house and one for the motorhome. I thought I was opening a shoe box. Twice. The point is, when we die, our stuff is left behind. All of it.

To make it easier for our children, each month Gerald and I tackle a new project. We let go of stuff that is out of date, expired, broken or no longer needed. And if Gerald ever needs a penis pump, we will put a warning label on the box, for the girls.

Jewelry can cause problems. Between sentimental value and the real value, deciding who gets what can cause undue tension. As the only daughter, my mother said over and over again, "I want Cindy to have my jewelry." It was one of her Alzheimer's broken record statements. Mom loved jewelry. Dad loved Mom. He bought her jewelry when he was in trouble, which was a lot! Ironically, I am not a jewelry person, and it never occurred to me to ignore my mother's wishes. Unfortunately, she did not put her request in writing, and my brothers did not honor her verbal wishes. Because I wasn't in touch with myself, who I was, I made emotional decisions that resulted in the purchase of many of her pieces at three times their value. It took me years to replace my regret for the emotional, financial waste with gratitude for the valuable lesson of self-discovery. If you are particular about who receives your jewelry, find out if they want it. If it's something you don't wear, why not give it away while you are alive to watch them enjoy wearing it now? If it is a piece you enjoy wearing yourself, contact your legal advisor about the best way to make this bequest.

Art can be another interesting area of contention. Supposedly, Mom and Dad had a piece of artwork that was museum quality, but none of the pieces appraised as such. Gerald has a collection of sand paintings he inherited from his mother. Growing up in New Mexico, she collected many beautiful examples of Native American art. Most of these pieces were created more than fifty years ago. If none of our daughters want to keep the collection together, rather than split it up, Gerald wants to locate a museum, university or other institution to donate these pieces. They aren't extraordinarily valuable, but together they are an impressive collection of art from another era.

Then, there are the family historical pieces that have been handed down for generations. Dishes, serving platters, marble doorknobs, walking canes. Pieces that you would never purchase but can't bring yourself to get rid of. If you love them, enjoy them. But if they are sitting in a box, forgotten, unappreciated, re-home them. Start with your children, then nieces, nephews, aunts, cousins, etc. I had a box of unmatched dishes that I took to my mother's sister. My aunt was ECSTATIC to receive the dishes. She made comments like, "Oh, I remember the cakes this plate served."

Finally, everyone's favorite stuff, pictures! I have boxes of pictures I inherited from my parents. The old smelly ones of people I don't know because they aren't labeled, as well as the pictures of us kids growing up, pictures of grandchildren, and their vacation photos. I have my own box of pictures of my youth, pictures of my children growing up, often duplicates of the ones from Mom's box, and my own grandchildren pictures. Gerald's box is smaller, but he has pictures from his parents and his daughter's childhood as well. This does not include the growing digital library. Pictures bring back memories and remind us of good times. They are difficult to throw away on a good day, impossible in the grip of grief. Do yourself and your children a favor by cleaning out your photo file together.

Develop Self-awareness

Earlier, I mentioned the plan to grow my businesses was to add passionate team members who use their strengths. Contained in this simple sentence are two impactful ideas that are worth extra consideration. *Passionate team member* indicates a depth of self-awareness that manifests itself in living with purpose and the ability to work well with others. *Use their strengths* indicates a knowledge of personal strengths and the ability to use them day to day.

In this Passing of the Torch stage, you will do the same for your heirs. Remember, this is an ongoing process. You're not passing the torch to them on Day One. You're training family members over a period of time, so they're ready when it's time to pass responsibilities to them. When you see life as your job, and your family as your business, you invest in their human capital development. Increase your family's skills by investing in training to help them identify their strengths, motives, personality, etc. Training in conflict resolution, nonviolent communication, emotional intelligence and other skills will help them discover their passion, work well together and live in their strengths.

"You don't owe any time in the future for mistakes made in the past."

—Ed Rush

Chapter Nine: Create the Vision

In the Foundation Phase, you discovered your top 5 values, and drafted a mission statement, vision statement, Capital Account Competency List, family story, and mantra in preparation for this step. The foundation you laid provides a starting point for your family to modify, which gives them the opportunity to take ownership of the Legacy Family Plan. In this next step, you and your family will co-create a vision for the future that the rising generation is excited to carry forward. This is the time to dream about who you want to become as a family, both now and in the future.

Create a New Story

Is it time to create a new story for your family? It is time to get to know each other for who your family members have become and accept each other in an authentic way? Growing up together doesn't mean you know someone. Many times, it's the complete opposite.

Before launching into the creation of a new vision, it's important for each family member to discover themselves first, and authentically accept each other. When siblings can let go of childhood hurts, remove rose-colored glasses, or pain goggles, and find common ground between different lifestyles, they are better prepared to communicate and trust each other after you are gone. Ideally, your family members like each other, but at a minimum, accepting each other and agreeing to respect each other now, WHILE YOU ARE ALIVE, will prepare them for the future when your stabilizing presence is gone.

Art, the estate liquidator who guided us through the process of distributing our parents' personal assets, helped me understand why my brothers had difficulty accepting my ideas. According to Art, they suffered from the "widdle sista syndrome." Having changed my diapers as a baby, they couldn't get past seeing me as their little sister. My Masters in Business degree, Texas Real Estate Broker license, years of experience working side-by-side with Dad, and good ideas didn't matter. My siblings had no idea who I had become as a person. We didn't have the ability to communicate or trust each other.

I filtered my middle brother's behavior through rose-colored glasses. After my parents were gone, my glasses were quickly wrenched away. Having spent a lifetime defending his actions, when my brother transferred his hatred from Dad to me, I was ill-prepared to face reality. He sees life through pain goggles and isn't even aware of their presence. Removing them isn't an option, because doing so would require him to let go of his victimhood. Over the past decade, I have learned to love him from afar, accept him for who he is, and maintain a healthy distance. Unfortunately, this means his son will never know his cousins, second cousins, or feel the love of an extended family.

The process of understanding yourself and accepting others is another lifelong, ongoing process. In our retreats, we lead families through a deep dive of self-discovery, then provide additional nuggets of information over time. It's like any form of knowledge, the more you learn, the less you know. On our website, we offer links to the core assessments for critical self-discovery that include StrengthFinders, The Color Code and 16 Personalities.

By leading your family through this process as a group, they have the opportunity to *experience an understanding* of each other by going through the process together. The reports provided by these assessments are rich conversation starters to understand how and why we respond to life based on our strengths, motives and personality. Judgment is replaced by understanding, which opens the door to creating a family-first vision of the future.

Remember when I spoke about hearing the two voices of my dad? They're back. I can hear the man I knew raising a ruckus about now. The idea of creating a new story has him madder than a wet hen, because it suggests the one he lived was wrong. Cuss words are flying. His lips are compressed in a thin white line. His eyes are narrowed to a slit, and his arms are across his chest in a tight self-embrace. I can practically see the steam coming from his ears.

Through the Color Code certification process, I realized Dad was motivated by power. According to Dr. Hartman, power is defined as motivation to get from Point A to Point B. There is nothing wrong with being motivated by power, it's what drove my dad to success. But, our motivations have strengths and limitations. As a family, we didn't know how to cope with the limitations of a strong power-motivated individual. Dad never had the opportunity to build his character to minimize the limitations of this power motivation.

Dad wasn't one to waste any time on regret and he was very intolerant of suggestions that he was wrong in any way. But my angel dad, the other voice, is urging me to share this solution and share his change of perspective. Now, he can see the strengths and limitations of the four Color Code motivations and how everyone, including him, can use the information to build character and work together. He has been through the fire, seen the destruction and made it to the other side. He knows Legacy Family Planning isn't about making anyone wrong; it's about understanding ourselves and accepting each other. Like me, he doesn't want others to suffer. Especially family leaders like him, who are motivated to get from A to B.

Before you co-create your family vision, schedule enough meetings to deep dive into self-discovery and acceptance with your family as a group. You'll be glad you did. And when the family is ready to move forward, retrieve your binders and complete Step Two of the Foundation Process with your family as a whole. You and your family are ready to create that shared vision.

Craft 5 Top Values, Family Mission, Vision, Family Story and Mantra

You will repeat the steps you completed in the second step of the Foundation Phase, except this time you will ask your entire family to participate. Each member of the family should complete the values exercise from Chapter 5 and narrow their list to their top 5 values. You can provide them with a copy of the worksheets, or ask them to download their own copy from our website at www.LegacyFamilyRevolution.com/LFWdownload.

Are there any shared values on everyone's lists? These values are the first to add to your legacy list. But what do you do if everyone's top 5 values are different? It's time for the group to make a joint decision, which is not always easy. You don't want the introverts to keep quiet while the extroverts take over. To encourage contributions from the entire group, I suggest using a structured method of group decision making called Nominal Group Technique (NGT). By the way, the nominal group technique is also appropriate for SWOT analysis, brainstorming and decision making.

This process is fun and energizing for the group by providing everyone with the opportunity to participate. Create one good sized sticky note for each value that appears on anyone's list. If "peace" shows up on multiple lists, you will only create one sticky note for it. Place the sticky notes on the walls around the room. Odds are, you will have almost every value from the list on the wall for this first round.

There will be two rounds of voting. The first round narrows the list to the top 10 values, and the second round narrows the list to the top 5 values. Voting is done with tiny dot stickers. Each member of the group receives five dot stickers for each round. Each dot represents one vote and can be used any way the family member chooses. One person may choose to put one vote on five different values, while another may choose to "stack the deck" by placing all five votes on one single value to potentially boost its ranking to make the cut to the next round.

Count the number of votes for each value, and narrow the number of values to ten. If there is a tie vote, you can increase the number.

The main goal is to narrow the number of choices for the second round.

Using the same voting method, narrow the values down to the top 5. Congratulations on a job well done! By now, your group may be fairly rowdy and ready for a break. When you reconvene, ask each family member to contribute their thoughts on the importance of each value and its impact on your family's future.

Once you have identified your revised top 5 values, it's time to review and edit the mission and vision statements. It is easier to edit than it is to create. By providing a draft version to work from, you have jump-started the process. Pre-set a time limitation for this exercise. You can always change your statements. Ideally, you will get them right from the start, but don't be concerned if, as you reach your time limit, the statements don't fully satisfy everyone in the group. These statements can take years to perfect. They are a work in progress.

The Capital Account Competency List will take time. Not only will you want to review the skills on each capital account list, you will brainstorm alternative training opportunities. Present the base list you created in the Foundation Phase and with their input. Grow the lists to reflect their interests. After you have co-created your list, discuss the budget for developing these skills for family members. Set SMART goals for accountability. SMART is an acronym for goals that are Specific, Measurable, Achievable, Realistic and Time-based. Remember to include the family founders on this list. Learning is a lifelong process, and if you feel you are proficient in all the listed skills, your list is not complete. This list is for everyone, including you.

In the Foundation Phase, you spent some time reflecting about a family story that will inspire future generations. Use this same technique to lead family members through your story selection process. If your family is rich in stories like mine is, you may end up using the nominal group technique to pick your family story! But if stories aren't your thing, just finding ***a story*** may be the challenge. But don't give up. Family stories are the glue that holds families together. Especially when you create a powerful mantra to go with it.

Your mantra should be short and memorable. Ideally it will start with a verb, and be no more than 3 to 5 words long. Your mantra is about taking action and being proactive. You can create mantras for all kinds of stories; don't feel like you have to limit yourself to one story. These mantras keep family stories alive.

One of my personal mantras came from my mother. After Dad passed away, every time I drove her in the car—more often than not, we were headed to a doctor's appointment—she would say, "See the sky, isn't it beautiful?" At the time I was irritated, because I wanted to have a "real" conversation with her. I wanted to know how she was feeling about Dad's absence. But her Alzheimer's brain was always focused on the sky. Before I picked her up, I anticipated the conversation and her parrot response, "See the sky, Cindy, isn't it beautiful?" I was angry and disappointed by my inability to connect with her in a meaningful way.

After Dad died, the cemetery association gave me permission to install a bench to sit on. I was surprised at the comfort I felt visiting the cemetery, and the bench gave me a nice place to sit. Shortly after Mom joined Dad, I took some flowers to place on their headstone. While sitting on the bench, I looked up. *I saw the sky* as if it were the first time. *It was beautiful.*

In that moment I realized the self-inflicted agony created by wanting Mom to live in my world after her Alzheimer's diagnosis. Had I understood my sweet mother's lessons at the time, I would have enjoyed our time together. Instead of resenting her inability to talk about things that didn't matter to her, I would have enjoyed the beauty of the sky with her and the lesson she was teaching me. No matter how small her world became, she found something to enjoy. She *showed* me how to enjoy life every day, and any time I need a reminder, I pause and *see the sky.*

Stories are powerful. There may come a time when you can't remember the name of this book. And if you don't implement the three phases, you certainly won't remember them. But, odds are, long after you read this book, you will remember the story of my mother. And, I hope when you need a boost, you too will take time to see the sky and enjoy its beauty.

Better yet, I pray you implement your Legacy Family Plan and co-create your vision for the future with your family. Discover the power of your own family story and mantra.

"The strength of the Constitution lies in the will of the people to defend it."
—Thomas Edison

Part Three
Creation Phase

*"The value of life is not in its duration,
but in its donation.
You are not important
because of how long you live,
you are important
because of how effective you live."*
—Myles Munroe

Chapter Ten: Your Legacy Family Plan

In this final phase, you will draft, adopt and implement a Legacy Family Plan. It will protect your family in ways that legal documents alone cannot. This process is effective, because your heirs are involved in the process. They are willing participants who learn how to communicate and trust each other through their participation in the process. The best legal minds in the estate planning industry cannot create a document that equals the impact of the group of documents you are about to create with your family.

Legal documents are not enough to protect your family, or your financial assets because traditionally, heirs are not involved in their creation. More often than not, heirs do not participate in the creation of legal documents and are not aware of the contents until after "IT" happens. Once the Cur$e of Inheritance has been unleashed, the majority of disputes are settled at the courthouse. The court system is clogged with unmerited lawsuits. No matter how well you craft a legal document, it can't stop someone from suing, with or without cause. Lawsuits don't just happen by themselves, they are filed by people. Unhappy people. Unless you are a celebrity like Prince or Howard Hughes who has acquaintances and "distant" relatives lining up to inherit, most wealth transfer disputes are filed by people who not only know each other, they once loved each other.

Legacy Planning is a preventative plan to protect your family's wealth. Rather than forcing heirs to adhere to a set of legal documents, they provide input into the process. Your Legacy Family Plan is a covenant that you are creating *with your family*. The term *covenant* is of Latin origin and means coming together (*con venire*). Your Legacy Family Plan is the living document that brings your family together. Actually, it is not just one document, it is a series of documents that provides governance, or decision making. These documents include your family's covenant, which consists of your mission statement, vision statement, top 5 values, family story and mantra, as well as your stewardship plan, strategic plan, shared asset plan, family bank, etc.

Draft the Plan

The first step in drafting your Legacy Family Plan is determining what documents you will need. Your vision and asset mix will help you determine the appropriate documents you will need to get started. Begin with the basics. You can always add documents to your plan as your needs change. As you go, make sure your documents are filed in your Legacy Drawer and ensure every family branch has a copy.

Before you begin the drafting process, review the Basic Principles, the 21 Key Characteristics, and discuss Cur$e of Inheritance prevention measures. Keep these guiding principles at the top of your mind as you draft your documents.

The Basic Principles

I have included a copy of my family's draft Capital Competency List for your consideration, and some clarifying questions to help you craft your Basic Principles. None of the principles are written in stone; please edit, add or delete, as needed, to create a list of Basic Principles and competencies your family can embrace.

1. *Your job is not your job. It's a vehicle to earn income. Your life is your job. Your job is to fully develop your unique potential and own your life.*

How are you developing your unique potential? Do you own your life, or does your life seem to own you? What is the single most important change you can make to improve your life?

2. *Your family is your business. The purpose of your business is to fully develop each family member's unique potential and teach them to own their life.*

How are you developing each family member's unique potential? Do they own their life, or are they trying to live up to expectations set by others? What one change can YOU make to help your family own their life?

3. *A consciousness mind-set is the key to success.*

How do you define consciousness? In your daily life, how do you practice consciousness?

4. *Each family member's authentic self is developed to realize his or her full potential. Inclusivity is the goal.*

How are family members encouraged to develop their authentic self? Are there any barriers to expressing their uniqueness?

5. *Provide safe opportunities to make mistakes. Learning from experience builds self-confidence and self-esteem.*

Are mistakes used as learning opportunities? How can mistakes be used to build self-confidence and self-esteem?

6. *Provide opportunities to defer instant gratification. It is a critical component of long-term success.*

What techniques do you use to delay gratification? How are you teaching this concept to your family?

7. *Think like a coach to prevent judgment and build curiosity. When questions are asked instead of making assumptions, it reduces conflict.*

When communicating with your family, what is your tendency? Do you make assumptions, or ask questions? What is the single most important change YOU can make to improve communication with your family?

8. *Maximize time spent in Stephen Covey's second quadrant of important but not urgent.*

Expressed as a percentage, how much time do you spend in the following quadrants?

important and urgent	_____%
important and not urgent	_____%
non-important and urgent	_____%
non-important and not urgent	_____%

9. *Everyone is doing their best.*

How you answer this question has been found to affect your belief about others. If you have trouble seeing yourself and others as doing their best, please read Brené Brown's groundbreaking book, *Rising Strong.*

10. *The strength of the family is determined by its weakest relationship. Improving this relationship is top priority.*

Your family is only as strong as its weakest member. Review your family member list and determine the weakest relationships. It could be any relationship: sibling, parent-child, husband-wife, or any other combination. Does anyone in your family suffer from abuse, addiction or untreated health issues? Ignoring these problems will not make them go away. Successful families do not try to tackle these challenges on their own, they employ help from professionals.

11. *The family's success relies on creating a foundational attitude of gratitude. It is the antidote for entitlement.*

Do family members feel entitled or grateful? How is gratitude practiced in your family?

12. *Your values create the framework for decisions in accordance with the family mission statement.*

What do you value and how do you share your values with your family? Naming a handful of values provides the guidance system for creating a meaningful Legacy Family Plan. In our workshops and retreats, we assist family leaders in narrowing down the list to create the framework they need to identify their unique family story, mission statement and stewardship plan.

13. *Your family story creates a unified family culture.*

What family story best exemplifies your values? If you have difficulty finding a story, or deciding which one is best, host a relaxed family meal and reminisce about good times, and hard times. After choosing your story, create a three-to-five-word statement that will be easy for future generations to remember. Examples include, "Red's got it." and "Five dollars in his pocket."

14. *Your mission statement provides clear guidance for investments in the four capital accounts.*

Now that you have your top values identified, it's time to create a mission statement. What is your mission statement?

15. *There are four capital accounts to invest in, both personally and as a family. The capital accounts include Financial, Intellectual, Social and Human.*

16. *Develop a list of competencies in the four capital accounts to provide a blueprint for a customizable educational plan.*

Use the sample list from the next section to create your list of competencies. This checklist provides the blueprint to train family members to master the skills they need to embody family values and achieve the family mission statement. Although Gerald and I made the list, and we are the family founders, we discovered many areas to further our education.

17. *Financial resources are invested to provide personalized competency training for family members.*

Successful Legacy Families see themselves as stewards of their financial assets, not owners. They accept responsibility to invest, grow and protect financial resources for the family's future. Most importantly, they train future generations to do the same, thereby growing the financial assets for an expanding number of family members. Do you consider yourself a steward of your resources? How are you teaching future generations to become stewards?

18. *Your formalized governance system provides the framework for making decisions.*

After you are gone, how will family members make decisions? Who will be allowed to vote, and under what circumstances?

19. *Get help. Children are more apt to listen to a "professional" instead of a parent.*

Successful families hire professionals to train their rising generation and create a "Board of Directors" (BOD). The BOD and the entire family meets on a regular basis to build relationships with the family founders and the rising generation. Legacy Family leaders have the courage to ask, "Is this the best person to assist my family after I am gone?" Who will be on your BOD?

20. *Be tenacious. Legacy Family Planning is a lifetime process that will have ups and downs. Focus on the positive results you are seeking.*

When you hit a bump in the road of life, and your adopted basic principles don't provide you with the tools you need to thrive, create a new principle.

Introduce Your Family to the 21 Key Characteristics

As a group, discuss each of the characteristics listed in Chapter 3 and ask: How will our plan be affected if we do incorporate this characteristic? How will our plan be affected if we do not incorporate this characteristic? How will we educate and provide experiences for the rising generation to embrace this characteristic?

Prevent the Cur$e

Minimize the conditions that unleash the Cur$e of Inheritance by recognizing the conditions in which it thrives. Remember, once "*IT*" is unleashed, you can't go back. Your family's involvement in the creation of your Legacy Family Plan will reduce jealousy, fear and selfishness. Although the environment of loss and grief will remain, you can prepare your heirs, replace entitlement with gratitude and create a family-first environment of cooperation and trust. Remember Buddy? The Cur$e of Inheritance can begin before you die.

The Cur$e of Inheritance is an ugly monster of jealousy, fear and selfishness that crushes families, eats money and destroys lives. The Cur$e of Inheritance is born in an environment of loss and grief, by unprepared heirs who feel entitled to unearned wealth and forget to see each other as human beings.

The Bill of Rights are the first ten amendments to the United States Constitution, but this single document is not sufficient to enforce the protection of these rights. We have detailed laws and regulations to protect the rights established in the Constitution.

At the family level, the documents you co-created in the previous step serve as your family's guiding light, similar to the Bill of Rights. Now, it's time to add additional documents, similar to laws and regulations that provide guidance for your family.

The best way to engage your family is to ask them to help. There are many pieces to put together when creating a Legacy Family Plan. Encourage participation by asking family members to research various parts of the plan, and present their ideas, so they become stakeholders in the process. Below is a list of documents most families will want to consider:

Documents to Consider

Family Covenant: This guiding document is the centerpiece of your plan. It is the written document that provides the rules and regulations for decision making, communication, conduct, privacy, conflict resolution and meeting frequency.

- Your Family Mission and Vision
- Definition of Terms
- Who qualifies as a family member?
- What happens after a divorce?
- Type of Governance System
- Responsibilities and Authority
- Evaluation
- Approval Processes
- What does fair mean?
- Care for Incapacitated Family Members
- Business Succession Planning
- Funding for Capital Account Competency List
- Compensation
- Code of Conduct
- Conflict Resolution
- Process for Changing the Plan
- Meeting Frequency

Strategic Plan: Your Strategic Plan is the "how-to" guide. SMART goals keep the plan moving. What measurements of success will be used? How will you determine when a course correction is necessary?

Stewardship Plan: In Chapter 6, you created a Stewardship Plan as part of your estate review. It's time to review this document with your family and make any necessary revisions.

Family Bank: Many families self-fund purchases of automobiles, homes, education and other expenses. Instead of paying interest to the bank, interest income increases the family wealth. This is not the charity portion of the estates. Funds borrowed from the family bank are expected to be paid back.

Shared Asset Plan: If you own time-shares, vacation homes, a business or other assets that created shared ownership, you will want to add a Shared Asset Plan to your document list.

Family Foundation: Many families create a family foundation to direct their social capital donations to ensure their desired outcome.

Creating a Governance System That Works

One of the main functions of your Legacy Family Plan is to provide governance for future generations. Governance is the action or manner of making a decision with authority. To better understand why most wealth transfers fail within three generations, let's trace how assets are governed as they are passed from one generation to another.

In the first generation, the wealth builder is a dictator making all the decisions. Upon transfer to the second generation, governance shifts to a partnership between children. This involuntary partnership is governed by legal documents prepared by the dictator. By the time the third generation receives the assets, governance shifts to a cousin consortium, which is, in essence, a bigger group of partners who have less in common than the previous owners using documents created decades before.

Your family covenant, or constitution, is the guiding document for decision making, replacing leaders, defining acceptable behaviors, establishing processes to resolve differences, and determining frequency of meetings and systems of accountability.

When family founders and the rising generation come together to create a governance plan, there is continuity from one generation to the next. Rather than directives handed down by a dictator, adult family members come together and create a transferable system of governance. Through their participation in the process, everyone has a stake in the outcome and is more likely to agree to abide by the plan. Instead of competing with each other, consensus is reached. This covenant, or family constitution, is a source of guidance for future generations to follow.

Success doesn't happen in a vacuum; every organization needs a leader. Your Legacy Family Plan will determine how leaders are selected, their responsibility and authority, as well as accountability and compensation, if any. This is not replacing the executor of your will, or any of the legal rights provided for in your legal documents. This is the leader of the family that ensures the values, mission and vision continues. This leader is often serving dual roles, one provided in legal documents, the other, from the Legacy Family Plan.

When Gerald and I moved to Boerne, we were 300 miles away from the girls. Having never moved away from my hometown area, this move was monumental for me. I needed the space to heal from the trauma of settling my parents' estate, and regroup mentally, physically and emotionally. Tiffany, my eldest daughter, suffered the most from our absence. She was quite vocal in missing us, and put forth effort to keep the family connected. Without being asked, she stepped into the role of family leader.

When heirs are not properly prepared, sibling leadership isn't easily accepted. Willingness to follow a parent's advice or instructions does not translate to listening to a sibling. Especially when they are the "widdle sista or kid brotha." *Providing the experience to work together* as a group, with the family founder's mentorship, is the key to the Legacy Family Planning process. Family members are trained to cooperate, and are prepared to accept their inheritance when they've had the opportunity to practice with the rising generation of Family Leadership.

Once the documents have been drafted, it's time to edit. Editing is the key to creating documents that build consensus. The goal is to create documents that your family is excited about adopting. This is a process, but the process provides the experience of working together as a team.

When you have a finalized draft of your entire Legacy Family Plan, invite your trusted advisors to review the draft. Are there changes in your estate plan that are needed to be made to support your Legacy Family Plan? Do your investments match your values? Do you need to refine your family covenant or mission statement? Together, work out the kinks in the draft stage so that adopting the documents seems seamless.

Adopt the Plan

Make your Adoption Meeting a very special occasion. Bring the whole family together, spouses and children included. Prepare a big family meal and break bread to celebrate adopting the plan you have created together. Adopting the plan together as a celebration of completing the process further unifies your family. Use technology to connect with family members who cannot attend, if possible. This is a momentous day for your family.

How will you preserve your document? Will each family receive their own copy? Once the plan has been made, how will you integrate it into your daily life? One of the best ideas came from a family friend who made business sized cards for everyone to carry a copy of the family mantra, values and mission statement in their billfold or wallet. Many families videotape their Legacy Plan, so future generations can see and hear their Family Founders.

Congratulations! Your Legacy Family Plan is in place. You have created three strong pillars to foster family relationships to create lasting wealth. But remember, lasting wealth is the by-product of family members who respect and like each other. The key to your family's success is your ability to transfer relationships from one generation to another. Simply put, lasting wealth is dependent on your ability to create a Legacy Family. One hundred years from now, future generations will bless you for your insight, commitment and vision. The good news is your Legacy Family Plan has benefits you can enjoy now. Celebrate as a family!

Implement the Plan

Now that your Legacy Family Plan has been adopted, you have the opportunity to enjoy the benefits. The Implementing-the-Plan stage is ongoing and will evolve as family assets grow, businesses start up and get sold, children grow up and get married, and grandchildren are born into the family. You will meet according to the schedule you established in your plan, evaluate the effectiveness of the plan, meet with your board of directors when necessary and continuously improve the plan. Review your plan with your advisors and update any legal documents as necessary. As you face challenges—and you will—you will find your Legacy Family Plan guiding you and your family through any challenges with confidence, so that you can live your legacy and become the living embodiment of your values. With a solid Legacy Family Plan in place, each day is a gift. Keep the 21 Key Characteristics, the Capital Account Competency List, and the Basic Principles handy to guide you through the process.

Become the Living Embodiment of Your Values

In our workshops and retreats we ask our participants to write a draft obituary. Some people are uncomfortable with this process before they write their draft. But afterward, they appreciate the insights and motivation it provides. When you have the courage to face your mortality, you discover what's really important, and realize that NOW is the time to achieve your aspirations. There are no guarantees for tomorrow. To write your draft obituary, write DRAFT at the top of the page, and let your creative juices flow. This is "a work of fiction based on a true story." Imagine your deepest desires coming true and include them in your draft AS IF every one of them had already happened. Take time to research accurate information of relatives that have passed, so that your children aren't scrambling for the correct information. Send your draft to your family. Encourage them to write their own. Have an obituary draft writing party! Writing a draft obituary brings a sense of urgency to making dreams come true.

Since implementing an annual obituary draft exercise in my New Year's Eve review, my life has been on a trajectory of satisfaction, motivation and joy. Putting into words how I want to be remembered helps me be that person. By living my values, I am becoming the person I want to be remembered for. Showing up congruent with my values makes me feel satisfied that I am doing my best. It may not always be easy, but it is rewarding. Accepting the mantle of leadership and taking the 100-year view have helped me keep my cool in some pretty intense moments. Moments that, in the past, would have resulted in hurt feelings, regret and subsequent apologies. Now, when I am in the midst of a challenge, I hear, "This too will pass." and look for a gracious solution.

Living with Confidence

One thing we can count on, the world around us is constantly changing. Those who are unprepared live in fear of change and have trouble adapting. When you live congruently with your values and embody the 21 Key Characteristics, you feel confident in your ability to thrive in any environment. The week before the presidential election, I accompanied Gerald to his doctor's appointment and while there, said "Hi" to the Physician's Assistant I see when I am in need of care. Michael mentioned how relieved he would be the following week. I had to ask, "Why?" He looked dumbfounded by my question, and responded, "The elections are next Tuesday." "Oh, sure," I said, and then launched into the benefits of Legacy Family Planning. As the matriarch of my Legacy Family, who won the election didn't really matter to me. I planned to cast my vote and accept the winner as our next president. I wasn't planning on wasting any of my precious energy on things beyond my control. I was busy taking action to move my business forward, enjoying my husband's company and preparing for a Thanksgiving feast with my family.

Living with a Legacy Family Plan in place, living your highest values, and having a 100-year view for the generations that follow empowers you to deal with life's ups and downs. Instead of fretting about things beyond your control, like changes in markets, economy, and who's running our nation's government, you strategize successful ways to navigate through the changes.

Living Your Legacy

You have created three strong pillars—Legal Documents, Legacy Family Plan and Financial Assets, etc.—to foster family relationships to create lasting wealth. It doesn't matter whether your goal is to enjoy your remaining time with your family, strengthen your family unity or build lasting wealth, Legacy Family Planning can positively impact your family now and in the future. Families are the smallest economic unit of society. Build your strong unit so that it can withstand internal and external pressures. One hundred years from now, future generations will bless you for your insight, commitment and vision.

About the Author

CINDY ARLEDGE, MBA is an author, speaker, trusted family advisor and visionary leader of the Legacy Family Revolution. Her company specializes in assisting business owners and financially successful families to create and implement their Legacy Family Plans. After surviving the destruction of her own family following her parents' deaths, Cindy vowed to help other families avoid common pitfalls that plague the majority of wealth transfer events.

Legacy Family Planning is a values-centered approach to estate planning that can significantly reduce wealth transfer failures. Legacy Family Planning focuses on fostering family relationships. Until now, it was reserved for ultra-wealthy families. As the smallest economic unit of society, Legacy Families are our nation's backbone of stability. Cindy's hope and dream is to lead a Legacy Family Revolution of one million families that have created a Legacy Family Plan. To reach her vision, Cindy knew it would take an army of experienced professionals. To meet the growing demand of this new industry, Cindy spearheaded the creation of the Legacy Family Planners Association (LFPA), an organization dedicated to training and certifying Legacy Family Planning professionals.

An active philanthropist, Cindy helped raise over $3 million to build a women's shelter in Boerne, TX. She divides her time between her Texas Hill Country ranch that she enjoys with her husband and her "crazy grandma" house in north Texas where she goes to play with her four grandchildren.

Please join the Revolution Now!

Website: http://www.LegacyFamilyRevolution.com

Facebook: http://www.Facebook.com/LegacyFamilyRevolution

LinkedIn: https://www.LinkedIn.com/in/cindyarledge

Amazon Author Page:
http://www.Amazon.com/author/cindyarledge

Website: http://www.LegacyFamilyPlannersAssociation.com

About the Illustrator

LISA ROTHSTEIN is the award-winning Madison Avenue ad agency copywriter and creative director best known for creating the famous "Wait'll We Get Our Hanes on You" campaign that changed America's underwear.

In her own creative consulting business, she uses a combo of cartooning and cutting-edge marketing strategy and language to help companies and entrepreneurs see their ideal clients and present their products, brand and message in a new and unforgettable way. She has both authored and illustrated Amazon best sellers in the business space. For creative consulting or cartoon projects: www.lisarothstein.com/cartoons

Hire a Legacy Family Planner to Speak at Your Event!

Are you looking for an attention-grabbing keynote speaker who will deliver a fresh new idea with a powerful message that adds to the long-term life success of your people?

Legacy Family Planning is the best-kept secret used by elite families who want to transfer values, character and wealth to future generations without the drama. Staggering to consider that, on average, more than half of your audience doesn't even have a Last Will & Testament.

Contact our office to **book a Legacy Family Speaker as your keynoter** and you're not only securing a profoundly impactful part of your program, you're investing in the long-term success of your people and their family's future.

For more info, visit
www.LegacyFamilyRevolution.com
or email us at info@legacyfamilyrevolution.com today.

Motivate and Inspire Others

Share a printed copy of this book.

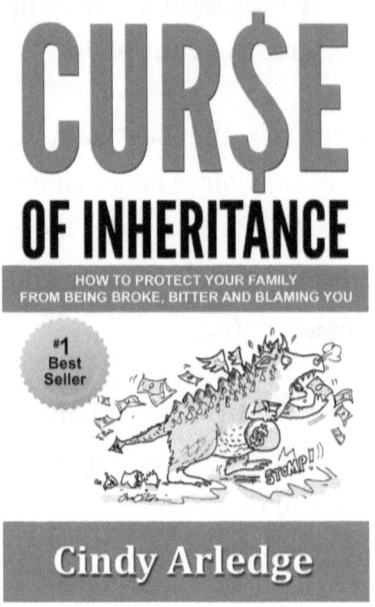

Amazon and BarnesandNoble.com

For bulk orders, contact us:
info@LegacyFamilyRevolution.com

www.LegacyFamilyRevolution.com

What would it be like to ENJOY walking 500 miles in 37 days?

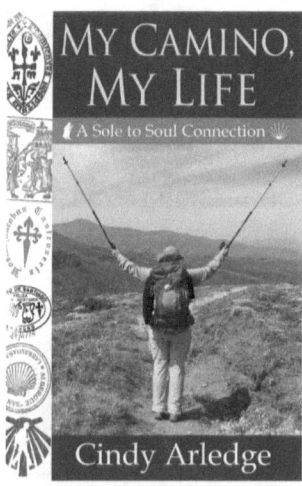

For thousands of years, Europeans have stepped out their front door and walked to Santiago, Spain. The purpose of this Pilgrimage, known as the Camino de Santiago, is to visit the bones of the Apostle James purported to be buried under the Cathedral. Like most Americans, Cindy was inspired to walk the Camino after watching *The Way*, a Hollywood movie released in 2011. Since then, an increasing number of Americans make up the 200,000+ Pilgrims who annually walk the Camino. Modern-day Pilgrims walk and bike the Camino for various reasons—from religious/spiritual to sport/outdoor appreciation.

Weeks before her departure, Cindy was plagued by plantar fasciitis and scheduled for unexpected surgery. Despite her physical challenges and inability to speak Spanish, Cindy set her intention to walk 500 miles with Ease and Grace, and always use indoor plumbing. In this memoir, Cindy shares her spellbinding story with intimacy and humor. Her positive approach to the hazards she encountered are inspiring and remarkable.

My Camino, My Life is available at
Amazon and BarnesandNoble.com

Are you seeking an exciting new business opportunity?
One that will help others?

Consider joining the growing number of professional advisors.

A Business with Purpose

For more information, contact:
210-414-7522
www.LegacyFamilyRevolution.com
info@LegacyFamilyRevolution.com

Notes

Notes

www.ingramcontent.com/pod-product-compliance
Lightning Source LLC
Chambersburg PA
CBHW020655300426
44112CB00007B/387